Ohio Legal Research

CAROLINA ACADEMIC PRESS
LEGAL RESEARCH SERIES

Suzanne E. Rowe, Series Editor

ೌ

Arizona, Second Edition—Tamara S. Herrera

Arkansas—Coleen M. Barger

California, Second Edition—Hether C. Macfarlane, Aimee Dudovitz
& Suzanne E. Rowe

Colorado—Robert Michael Linz

Connecticut—Jessica G. Hynes

Federal, Second Edition—Mary Garvey Algero, Spencer L. Simons,
Suzanne E. Rowe, Scott Childs & Sarah E. Ricks

Florida, Fourth Edition—Barbara J. Busharis, Jennifer LaVia
& Suzanne E. Rowe

Georgia—Nancy P. Johnson, Elizabeth G. Adelman & Nancy J. Adams

Idaho, Second Edition—Tenielle Fordyce-Ruff & Kristina J. Running

Illinois, Second Edition—Mark E. Wojcik

Iowa—John D. Edwards, M. Sara Lowe, Karen L. Wallace
& Melissa H. Weresh

Kansas—Joseph A. Custer & Christopher L. Steadham

Kentucky—William A. Hilyerd, Kurt X. Metzmeier & David J. Ensign

Louisiana, Second Edition—Mary Garvey Algero

Massachusetts—E. Joan Blum

Michigan, Second Edition—Pamela Lysaght & Cristina D. Lockwood

Minnesota—Suzanne Thorpe

Mississippi—Kristy L. Gilliland

Missouri, Third Edition—Wanda M. Temm & Julie M. Cheslik

New York, Third Edition—Elizabeth G. Adelman, Theodora Belniak,
Courtney L. Selby & Brian T. Detweiler

North Carolina, Second Edition—Scott Childs & Sara Sampson

Ohio, Second Edition—Sara Sampson, Katherine L. Hall
& Carolyn Broering-Jacobs

Oklahoma—Darin K. Fox, Darla W. Jackson & Courtney L. Selby

Oregon, Third Edition—Suzanne E. Rowe

Pennsylvania—Barbara J. Busharis & Bonny L. Tavares

Tennessee—Sibyl Marshall & Carol McCrehan Parker

Texas, Revised Printing—Spencer L. Simons

Washington, Second Edition—Julie Heintz-Cho, Tom Cobb
& Mary A. Hotchkiss

West Virginia—Hollee Schwartz Temple

Wisconsin—Patricia Cervenka & Leslie Behroozi

Wyoming—Debora A. Person & Tawnya K. Plumb

ೌ

Ohio Legal Research

Second Edition

Sara Sampson
Katherine L. Hall
Carolyn Broering-Jacobs

Suzanne E. Rowe, Series Editor

CAROLINA ACADEMIC PRESS

Durham, North Carolina

Library of Congress Cataloging-in-Publication Data

Sampson, Sara, author.
  Ohio legal research / Sara Sampson, Katherine L. Hall, and Carolyn Broering-Jacobs. -- Second edition.
      pages cm -- (Carolina Academic Press legal research series)
  Includes bibliographical references and index.
  ISBN 978-1-61163-749-6 (alk. paper)
  1. Legal research--Ohio. I. Hall, Katherine L., author. II. Broering-Jacobs, Carolyn, author. III. Title.
  KFO75.S26 2015
  340.072'0771--dc23
                                    2015028501

CAROLINA ACADEMIC PRESS
700 Kent Street
Durham, North Carolina 27701
Telephone (919) 489-7486
Fax (919) 493-5668
www.cap-press.com

Printed in the United States of America
2018 Printing

Summary of Contents

List of Tables and Figures   xv

Series Note   xix

Preface and Acknowledgments   xxi

Chapter 1 · The Research Process and Legal Analysis   3

Chapter 2 · Researching Constitutions   15

Chapter 3 · Researching Statutes   23

Chapter 4 · Understanding Cases   35

Chapter 5 · Finding and Updating Cases   49

Chapter 6 · Researching Court Rules and Documents   69

Chapter 7 · Researching Administrative Law   77

Chapter 8 · Researching Local Law   89

Chapter 9 · Researching Secondary Sources   93

Chapter 10 · Researching Legislative History   107

Chapter 11 · Research Strategies   125

Chapter 12 · Legal Citation   133

Appendix A · Ohio Research Guides   161

Appendix B · Important Legal Research Terminology and Abbreviations 165

Appendix C · County and Law School Libraries in Ohio   171

Appendix D · Selected Legal Writing and Research Texts   177

About the Authors   179

Index   181

Contents

List of Tables and Figures   xv

Series Note   xix

Preface and Acknowledgments   xxi

Chapter 1 · The Research Process and Legal Analysis   3

I. Legal Research Generally   3

II. The Intersection of Legal Research and Legal Analysis   3

III. Types of Legal Authority   4

IV. Court Systems   5
    A. Ohio Courts   5
    B. Federal Courts   7
    C. Courts of Other States   8

V. Overview of the Research Process   9
    A. Generating Research Terms   10
    B. Researching the Law — Organization of This Text   11

VI. Selecting Online Sources for Legal Research   12

Chapter 2 · Researching Constitutions   15

I. Constitutions Generally   15

II. The Ohio and U.S. Constitutions   15
    A. Constitutional Rights   15
    B. Unconstitutional Legislation   16
    C. Other Constitutional Provisions   16

III. Constitutional Amendments   17

IV. Researching the Ohio and U.S. Constitutions   17
     A. Find a Secondary Source for an Overview   18
     B. Find the Relevant Text of the Ohio or U.S. Constitution   18
     C. Find Cases That Construe or Apply the Constitution   19
     D. Update the Constitutional Provision   20
     E. Research the History of a Constitutional Provision or
         Constitutional Amendment   21

V. Citing Constitutions   21

VI. Additional Resources   22

Chapter 3 · Researching Statutes   23

I. Statutes Generally   23

II. Ohio Statutes   23
     A. Session Laws   24
     B. Statutory Codes   24
     C. Annotated Statutory Codes   25

III. Federal Statutes   25
     A. Session Laws   27
     B. Statutory Codes   27
     C. Annotated Statutory Codes   28

IV. Statutory Research Process   28
     A. Develop a List of Research Terms   28
     B. Consult Secondary Sources for an Overview and Citations to
         Primary Authority   29
     C. Find and Read the Statutory Language   29
     D. Find Cases that Interpret or Apply the Statute   30
     E. Updating Statutes   30

V. Other Research Tools   31
     A. Uniform Laws and Model Acts   31
     B. Statutory Surveys   32
     C. Archived Codes   32

VI. Citing Statutes   33

Chapter 4 · Understanding Cases   35

I. Cases and Court Reporters Generally   35

II. Publication of Ohio Cases   36
    A. Official Publication   36
    B. Print Published and Non-Print Published Distinction   37
    C. Unofficial Print Publication   38

III. Reporters for Federal Cases   38

IV. Topical Reporters   40

V. Online Commercial Sources for Cases   40

VI. Features of a Case   41

VII. Reading and Analyzing Cases   44
    A. Brief Overview of Civil Procedure   44
    B. Analyzing the Substance of the Case   45
    C. Strategies for Reading Cases   47

Chapter 5 · Finding and Updating Cases   49

I. Researching Cases Generally   49

II. Full-Text Searching   50
    A. Types of Searches   50
    B. Narrowing Results with Limits or Filters   52
    C. Choosing What to Read   52

III. Online Subject Searching   53
    A. Topical Searching on WestlawNext   53
      1. West's Key Number Digest   53
      2. Practice Areas   54
    B. Topical Searching on Lexis Advance   54

IV. Starting with a Relevant Case   55

V. Using Words and Phrases   55

VI. Updating Cases with Citators   56

VII. Citing Cases   60

Appendix: West Print Digests   60
    1. Searching for a Legal Issue with the Descriptive-Word Index   63

2. Starting with a Relevant Case   66
3. Words & Phrases   66
4. Table of Cases   67

Chapter 6 · Researching Court Rules and Documents   69

I. Court Rules and Court Documents Generally   69

II. Ohio and Federal Court Rules   69

III. Researching Court Rules   70
A. Develop a List of Research Terms   71
B. Find and Read the Rule   71
C. Find Cases that Interpret or Apply the Rule   72
D. Update the Rule   73

IV. Citing Court Rules   73

V. Rules of Professional Conduct   74

VI. Finding Court Documents   74

Chapter 7 · Researching Administrative Law   77

I. Administrative Law Generally   77

II. Researching Administrative Rules and Regulations   78
A. General Approaches to Researching Administrative Rules   79
B. Researching Ohio Rules   80
1. Ohio Administrative Code   80
2. *Ohio Monthly Record* and the *Register of Ohio*   82
3. Updating Ohio Rules   82
C. Researching Federal Regulations   83
1. *Code of Federal Regulations*   83
2. *Federal Register*   84
3. Updating Federal Regulations   86

III. Researching Administrative Decisions   86
A. Accessing Agency Decisions   86
B. Updating Agency Decisions   87

IV. Citing Administrative Rules and Decisions   87
A. Rules and Regulations   87
B. Agency Decisions   88

Chapter 8 · Researching Local Law 89

I. Local Law Generally 89

II. Finding Municipal Codes 90

III. Updating Municipal Codes 91

IV. Citing Municipal Codes 91

Chapter 9 · Researching Secondary Sources 93

I. Secondary Sources Generally 93

II. Legal Encyclopedias 93

III. Practice Treatises 95

IV. Forms 96
   A. Ohio Forms 97
   B. Federal Forms 97
   C. General Forms 98

V. Law Journals, Legal Newsletters, and Blogs 98
   A. Law Journals 98
   B. Legal Newsletters 99
   C. Legal Blogs 100

VI. Jury Instructions 101

VII. General Secondary Sources 102
   A. *American Law Reports* 102
   B. Restatements and Principles — American Law Institute 103
   C. Uniform Laws and Model Acts 105

VIII. Citing Secondary Sources 106

Chapter 10 · Researching Legislative History 107

I. Legislative History Generally 107

II. Overview of the Legislative Process 108
   A. Bill Introduced 108
   B. Committee Activity 109
   C. Floor Activity 109
   D. Executive Activity 109

III. Federal Legislative History   110
      A. Types of Federal Legislative History Documents   110
      B. Sources for Federal Legislative History Documents   111
          1. Fee-Based Sources Online   111
          2. Free Sources Online   112
          3. Print Sources   112
      C. Finding Federal Legislative History Documents   114
      D. Tracking Current Federal Legislation   116
          1. Using Congress.gov to Track Federal Legislation   116
          2. Other Online Sources for Tracking Federal Legislation   116
              a. Govtrack.us   116
              b. WestlawNext   116
              c. Lexis Advance   117
              d. Bloomberg Law   117

IV. Ohio Legislative History   117
      A. Types of Ohio Legislative History Documents   117
      B. Sources of Ohio Legislative History Documents   118
          1. Fee-Based and Free Sources Online   119
          2. Print Sources   119
      C. Finding Ohio Legislative History Documents   119
      D. Tracking Ohio Legislation   120
          1. Govtrack.us   121
          2. WestlawNext   121
          3. Lexis Advance   121
          4. Hannah Capitol Connection   122
          5. Gongwer   122

V. Citing Legislative History Documents   122

Chapter 11 · Research Strategies   125

I. Legal Research Process   125

II. Research Example   126
      A. Generating Research Terms   126
      B. Consulting Secondary Sources   127
      C. Finding Statutes and Regulations   129
      D. Finding Cases   129
      E. Updating Authorities   130
      F. Concluding Your Research   131

Chapter 12 · Legal Citation   133

I. Introduction to Legal Citation   133
  A. The Purpose of Legal Citation   133
  B. Sources of Citation Rules   134
  C. Incorporating Citations into a Document   135
  D. Citations to Print and Online Versions   136

II. *Ohio Manual of Citations*   137
  A. General Instructions for Citing Cases Under the
    Ohio Manual of Citations   137
    1. Party Names   138
    2. Reporters   138
    3. Parentheticals   138
    4. Pinpoint Citations   139
    5. Introductory Signals   139
    6. Prior and Subsequent History   140
  B. Special Rules for Citing Particular Types of Ohio Cases   141
    1. Citing Ohio Cases Decided Before May 1, 2002   141
      a. Print Published (Reported) Cases   141
      b. Cases Not Appearing in a Print Reporter   142
    2. Citing Ohio Cases Decided After May 1, 2002   142
      a. Print Published Cases   143
      b. Non-Print Published Cases   144
  C. Citing Cases from Other State Jurisdictions   145
  D. Citing Cases from Federal Courts   146
  E. Citing Statutes and Regulations   146
  F. Secondary Sources   147
  G. Short-Form Citations   147

III. The *Bluebook* and *ALWD Guide*   147
  A. Citations for Practice Documents   149
    1. *Bluebook* Quick Reference Guides   149
    2. Index   149
  B. Cases   150
    1. Essential Components of Case Citations   150
    2. Full and Short Citations to Cases   151
    3. Prior and Subsequent History   153
  C. Codes   153
  D. Constitutions   155
  E. Secondary Sources   155

F. Signals   155
G. Quotations   156
H. Citation Details   157
I. Citations for Law Review Articles   158

IV. Editing Citations   159

V. Deciphering Legal Abbreviations   159

Appendix A · Ohio Research Guides   161

I. Online Ohio Research Guides   161

II. Print Research Guides   163

Appendix B · Important Legal Research Terminology and Abbreviations 165

Appendix C · County and Law School Libraries in Ohio   171

Appendix D · Selected Legal Writing and Research Texts   177

About the Authors   179

Index   181

List of Tables and Figures

Tables

Table 1-1. Examples of Authority in Ohio Research   5

Table 1-2. Overview of the Research Process   9

Table 1-3. Generating Research Terms   11

Table 2-1. Outline of Constitutional Law Research   18

Table 2-2. Ohio Constitution Citation Example   21

Table 3-1. Chapters in Title 43, Liquors   24

Table 3-2. Overview of the Ohio Statutory Research Process 28

Table 3-3. Sections of Chapter 1101, Banks — Offenses   30

Table 3-4. Ohio Statute Citation Example   33

Table 3-5. Federal Statute Citation Example   33

Table 4-1. State Cases Included in Regional Reporters   38

Table 4-2. Reporters for Federal Court Cases   39

Table 5-1. Connectors and Commands for Online Searching 51

Table 5-2. Outline for Updating Cases   56

Table 5-3. Selected Signals of Online Citators   58

Table 5-4. Selected Types of Treatment in Online Citators 59

Table 5-5. Ohio Case Citation Examples   60

Table 5-A. Selected Digests   63

Table 6-1. Selected Court Rules Applicable to Ohio Courts   70

Table 6-2. Overview of Court Rules Research Process   71

Table 6-3. Examples of Court Rule Citation   74

Table 7-1. Example of the Relationship Between a Statute and Rules   79

Table 7-2. Regulation Citation Example   88

Table 8-1. Commercial Publishers of Municipal Codes   90

Table 8-2. Municipal Code Citation   91

Table 9-1. List of *Baldwin's Ohio Practice* Treatises   95

Table 9-2. List of LexisNexis's Ohio Practice Treatises   96

Table 9-3. Examples of *American Law Reports* Annotations   103

Table 9-4. Restatement Topics   104

Table 9-5. Principles Subjects   104

Table 9-6. Citation Examples for Secondary Sources   106

Table 10-1. Sources for Online Legislative History   113

Table 10-2. Online Sources for Ohio Legislative History   120

Table 10-3. Ohio Bill Citation Example   122

Table 10-4. Federal House Report Citation Example   123

Table 11-1. Overview of the Research Process   125

Table 11-2. Generating Research Terms   126

Table 12-1. Citation Example   134

Table 12-2. Citation Information Important to Legal Researchers   135

Table 12-3. Examples of Citation Sentences and Citation Clauses   136

Table 12-4. Structure of the *Ohio Manual of Citations*   137

Table 12-5. Signals in the *Ohio Manual*   140

Table 12-6. Example Ohio Reported Cases Decided Before May 1, 2002   141

Table 12-7. Example Ohio Unreported Cases Decided Before May 1, 2002   142

Table 12-8. Excerpt from an Ohio Supreme Court Opinion   143

Table 12-9. Example Ohio Print Published Cases Decided After
    May 1, 2002 144

Table 12-10. Example Ohio Non-print Published Cases Decided On or
    After May 1, 2002 145

Table 12-11. Example Federal Case Citations 146

Table 12-12. Example Code Citations 146

Table 12-13. Citations to Secondary Sources 147

Table 12-14. Structure of the *Bluebook* and the *ALWD Guide* 148

Table 12-15. Examples of Reported Cases in *Bluebook*/*ALWD* Citation 151

Table 12-16. Examples of Full Citations 152

Table 12-17. Examples of Statutory and Regulatory Code Citations 154

Table 12-18. Examples of Constitutional Citations 155

Table 12-19. Secondary Source Citations in *Bluebook*/*ALWD* Form 155

Table 12-20. Common *Bluebook*/*ALWD* Signals 156

Table 12-21. *Bluebook*/*ALWD* Typeface for Law Review Footnotes 158

Figures

Figure 1-1. Ohio Court Structure 7

Figure 2-1. Excerpt from the Constitution of the State of Ohio from
    WestlawNext 20

Figure 3-1. Excerpt from *Baldwin's Ohio Revised Code Annotated* 26

Figure 4-1. Excerpt of Ohio Case from *Ohio State Reports* 42

Figure 5-A. Excerpt from a Case in West's *North Eastern Reporter* 61

Figure 5-B. Excerpts from *West's Ohio Digest* "Adoption" 62

Figure 5-C. Excerpts from the Descriptive-Word Index in *West's
    Ohio Digest* 64

Figure 5-D. Excerpts from *West's Ohio Digest* Analysis for Adoption 65

Figure 5-E. Excerpt from Words & Phrases in *West's Ohio Digest* 66

Figure 6-1. Sample Court Docket 75

Figure 7-1. Branches of Government 78

Figure 7-2. Example of an Ohio Rule in the Ohio Administrative Code 81

Figure 7-3. Sample Federal Regulation in the CFR 83

Figure 7-4. Excerpt from the *Federal Register* Table of Contents 85

Figure 8-1. Sample Municipal Ordinance 90

Figure 9-1. Excerpt from *Ohio Jurisprudence 3d* 94

Figure 10-1. Legislative Process 107

Figure 10-2. History Note in *United States Code* 114

Figure 10-3. Bill Summary on Congress.gov 115

Figure 10-4. History Note for Ohio Statute 121

Figure 11-1. *Ohio Jurisprudence 3d*, Family Law 127

Series Note

The Legal Research Series published by Carolina Academic Press includes titles from states around the country as well as a separate text on federal legal research. The goal of each book is to provide law students, practitioners, paralegals, college students, laypeople, and librarians with the essential elements of legal research in each jurisdiction. Unlike more bibliographic texts, the Legal Research Series books seek to explain concisely both the sources of legal research and the process for conducting legal research effectively.

Preface and Acknowledgments

Ohio Legal Research provides a concise introduction to Ohio-specific primary authorities and research tools for readers new to legal research or new to researching Ohio law. *Ohio Legal Research* introduces federal resources alongside their Ohio counterparts, which makes the text useful for an introductory research course that covers both state and federal research. Written with the understanding that research is best learned by practice, *Ohio Legal Research* offers succinct explanation to guide the novice without including so much as to overwhelm.

Ohio Legal Research follows a pragmatic process-based approach by introducing the sources of law and a process for researching those sources in Chapter 1. Subsequent chapters then employ that research process to explain how to research constitutions, statutes, cases, court rules, administrative law, and legislative history (Chapters 2 through 8, and 10). Chapter 9 covers secondary sources. Chapter 11 pulls process and substance together by walking the reader through researching a legal issue following the research process used throughout the text.

This updated second edition incorporates recent changes to the major electronic research platforms, while maintaining a process focus that will help the reader no matter which platform is available. Updated web addresses also point the researcher to many materials available for free online, including the recently adopted, official electronic reporting system for Ohio case law. Finally, *Ohio Legal Research* includes a fully revised chapter on citation that teaches basic citation form using the major citation manuals and, perhaps most significant to the Ohio practitioner, the recently overhauled *Ohio Manual of Citations* (Chapter 12).

We are indebted to Suzanne Rowe for her editorial guidance in writing this book. Her editorial assistance was as valuable in the second edition as it was in the first. Chapters 1, 4, 12, and the appendix to Chapter 5 are based in part upon her book *Oregon Legal Research*. Many thanks to her team for its help in editing the book, especially Sarah Garrott, Ariana Denley, and Corina Ubario.

In this second edition, we welcome a new co-author, Carolyn Broering-Jacobs, who has added her expertise in Ohio legal research and writing to this edition.

We remain grateful to those who helped with the first edition of the book, authored by Katherine Hall and Sara Sampson. The staffs of the Moritz Law Library at The Ohio State University and of the Georgetown University Law Library provided invaluable assistance. Special thanks to Matt Steinke, now at University of Texas, for his expert advice and to Intaba Shauri, former Georgetown Law research assistant, for his exceptional help on this project.

We also wish to thank our families and friends for their support.

Ohio Legal Research

Chapter 1

The Research Process and Legal Analysis

I. Legal Research Generally

The fundamentals of legal research are the same in every American jurisdiction; however, the details often vary. While some variations are minor, others are more significant and require specialized knowledge of the available resources and the analytical framework in which those resources are used. This book focuses on the resources and analysis required to be thorough and effective in researching Ohio law. The focus on Ohio law is supplemented with brief explanations of federal research and research into the law of other states, both to introduce other resources and to highlight some of the variations.

II. The Intersection of Legal Research and Legal Analysis

Legal analysis is an integral part of the legal research process. The basic steps in legal research are simple: identify legal issues and search terms, search the appropriate legal source to find the applicable law, and then update the law to make sure it is current. However, once the necessary legal analysis is interwoven throughout this process, legal research often proves complicated and challenging.

The legal analysis of a research issue raises numerous questions. What type of source should you search? Which words or terms should you use in searching the selected source's index or full-text database? After reading the text of a retrieved document, how will you determine whether it is relevant to your client's situation? How will you determine whether more recent material changed the law or merely applied it in a new situation? The answer to each of these questions requires legal analysis. This intersection of research and analysis can make legal research very difficult, especially for the novice. While this book focuses on legal research, it also addresses the fundamental aspects of legal analysis required to conduct research competently.

III. Types of Legal Authority

Before researching the law, you must be clear about the goal of your research. In every research situation, you want to find constitutional provisions, statutes, administrative rules, and judicial opinions that control your client's situation. In other words, you are searching for primary, mandatory authority.

In legal research, the type and level of authority of a legal source are fundamental issues. The two types of legal authority are primary and secondary. *Primary authority* is law produced by government bodies with law-making power. Legislatures enact statutes; courts write judicial opinions; and administrative agencies promulgate rules (also called regulations). *Secondary authority* includes all other legal sources, such as treatises, law review articles, and legal encyclopedias. These secondary sources are designed to assist you in understanding and analyzing the law and locating primary authority, but they are not themselves the law.

A legal resource's level of authority is characterized as either mandatory or persuasive. *Mandatory authority* is binding on the court that would hear the case if it was litigated. In a question of Ohio law, mandatory or binding authority includes Ohio's constitution, statutes enacted by the Ohio legislature, opinions of the Supreme Court of Ohio,[1] and Ohio administrative rules. *Persuasive authority* is not binding, but may be followed if relevant and well reasoned. Authority may be merely persuasive if it is from a different jurisdiction or if it is not itself a court opinion, statute, or administrative regulation. For an Ohio court applying an Ohio statute, examples of persuasive authority include a similar Illinois statute, an opinion of a Michigan state court, and a law review article. Notice in Table 1-1 that persuasive authority may be either primary or secondary authority, while mandatory authority is always primary.

---

1. An opinion from an Ohio Court of Appeals is binding on the trial courts within its jurisdiction if the Supreme Court of Ohio has not addressed the legal question at issue. *See Hudson Distribs. v. Eli Lilly & Co.*, 209 N.E.2d 234, 240 (Ohio C.P. 1965).

Table 1-1. Examples of Authority in Ohio Research

	Mandatory Authority	**Persuasive Authority**
Primary Authority	Ohio statutes Ohio Supreme Court cases	Illinois statutes Michigan Supreme Court cases
Secondary Authority	—	Law review articles Restatements of the law Treatises Legal encyclopedias

Within mandatory authority, there is an interlocking hierarchy of law involving constitutions, statutes, administrative rules, and judicial opinions. The constitution of each state is the supreme law of that state. If a statute is on point, that statute comes next in the hierarchy, followed by administrative rules. Judicial opinions may interpret a statute or rule, but they cannot disregard it. A judicial opinion may, however, decide that a statute violates the constitution or that a rule goes beyond what an agency is permitted to do. If there is no constitutional provision, statute, or administrative rule on point, the issue will be controlled by *common law,* also called judge-made law.

IV. Court Systems

Because legal research often involves reading judicial opinions, researchers need to understand the court system. The basic court structure includes a trial court, intermediate courts of appeals, and an ultimate appellate court, usually called the "supreme" court. These courts exist at both the state and federal levels.

A. Ohio Courts

In Ohio, the trial court system consists of several different types of courts:

- Courts of Common Pleas
- Municipal Courts
- County Courts
- Mayor's Courts
- Court of Claims

Each type of trial court handles certain types of cases.

The Courts of Common Pleas, established under the Ohio Constitution, are Ohio's main trial courts.[2] There are currently 88 of these courts, which handle most civil and criminal cases along with domestic relations, juvenile, and probate proceedings. These courts also hear appeals from decisions of some Ohio administrative agencies.

The subject matter jurisdiction[3] of the other trial courts is more limited. The Municipal and County Courts hear criminal misdemeanor and traffic cases along with civil cases not exceeding $15,000.[4] Mayor's Courts hear only cases involving traffic or municipal ordinance violations.[5] Convictions in a Mayor's Court may be appealed to the Municipal or County Court.[6] The Court of Claims hears civil actions against the State of Ohio.[7] Currently, there are 125 Municipal Courts, 41 County Courts, over 300 Mayor's Courts, and a single Court of Claims.

Ohio's intermediate appellate courts, called the Courts of Appeals, were created by the Ohio Constitution.[8] The Courts of Appeals are divided into 12 districts located throughout the state, each consisting of a panel of three judges. They hear appeals from decisions of Ohio's trial courts as well as appeals from decisions of certain Ohio administrative agencies. The Courts of Appeals have original jurisdiction in certain proceedings, including mandamus, habeas corpus, and quo warranto proceedings.[9]

The Supreme Court of Ohio, established under the Ohio Constitution, is the court of last resort.[10] The court is composed of seven elected justices. The justices sit *en banc* to hear all cases, unless a justice is recused. The court mainly hears appeals from decisions of the Ohio Courts of Appeals. It also hears appeals directly from the Courts of Common Pleas of death sentences and from certain administrative agency actions. The Supreme Court of Ohio has original jurisdiction in the same matters as do the Courts of Appeals, in addition to jurisdiction over attorney practice and membership in the bar.

---

2. Ohio Const. art. IV, § 4.

3. Subject matter jurisdiction limits the kind of cases a court can decide (e.g., in Ohio, Common Pleas courts have subject matter jurisdiction over felony criminal cases).

4. *See* Ohio Rev. Code Ann. §§ 1901.17–1901.18, 1907.02–1907.03 (West 2014).

5. *See* Ohio Rev. Code Ann. § 1905.01(A)–(C) (West 2014).

6. Ohio Rev. Code Ann. § 1905.22 (West 2014).

7. Ohio Rev. Code Ann. § 2743.03(A) (West 2006).

8. Ohio Const. art. IV, § 3.

9. Ohio Const. art. IV, § 3(B)(1)(a), (b), (c).

10. Ohio Const. art. IV, § 2.

Figure 1-1 shows the hierarchy of Ohio state courts. The Ohio judiciary's website contains a wealth of information on Ohio courts, including a map of Ohio's judicial districts, links to individual court websites, an explanation of the jurisdiction of state courts, lists of court personnel, and recent court opinions.[11]

Figure 1-1. Ohio Court Structure

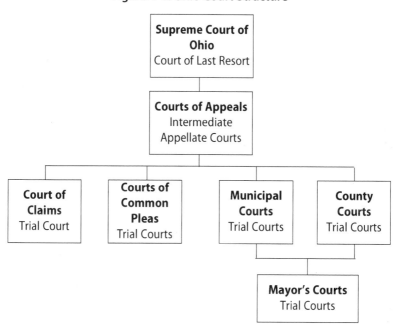

B. Federal Courts

In the federal judicial system, the trial courts are called United States District Courts. There are 94 district courts in the federal system, with each district drawn from a particular state.[12] Ohio is divided into two districts: the United States District Court for the Northern District of Ohio and the United States District Court for the Southern District of Ohio. Both the Northern and the Southern Districts are further divided into Eastern and Western divisions. The Northern District's Eastern Division is located in Cleveland, Youngstown, and Akron; the Western Division is in Toledo. The Southern District's Eastern

---

11. The Ohio Supreme Court's website can be accessed at www.sconet.state.oh.us.

12. In addition to the federal district courts, there are two subject-specific federal trial courts: the Court of International Trade and the U.S. Court of Federal Claims.

Division is located in Columbus; the Western Division sits in Dayton and Cincinnati.

Intermediate appellate courts in the federal system are called United States Courts of Appeals. There are courts of appeals for each of the thirteen federal circuits. Twelve of these circuits are based on geographic jurisdiction. In addition to eleven numbered circuits covering all the states, there is the District of Columbia Circuit. The thirteenth federal circuit, called the Federal Circuit, hears appeals from district courts in all other circuits on issues related to patent law and from certain specialized courts and agencies. A map showing the federal circuits is available online.[13]

Ohio is in the Sixth Circuit. This means that cases from the United States District Court for the Northern and Southern Districts of Ohio are appealed to the United States Court of Appeals for the Sixth Circuit. This circuit encompasses Kentucky, Michigan, Ohio, and Tennessee.

The highest court in the federal system is the United States Supreme Court. It decides cases concerning the United States Constitution and federal statutes. This court does not have the final say on matters of purely state law; that authority rests with the highest court of each state. Parties who wish to have the U.S. Supreme Court hear their case must file a petition for *certiorari*, as the court has discretion over which cases it hears.

The website for the federal judiciary contains maps, court addresses, explanations of jurisdiction, and other helpful information.[14]

C. Courts of Other States

Most states have the three-tier court system of Ohio and the federal judiciary. A few states do not have an intermediate appellate court, such as Montana and West Virginia. Another difference in some court systems is that the "supreme" court is not the highest court. In New York, the trial courts are called supreme courts and the highest court is the Court of Appeals. Two other states, Massachusetts and Maine, call their highest courts the Supreme Judicial Court.

---

13. *See* www.uscourts.gov/court-locator.
14. The address is www.uscourts.gov.

V. Overview of the Research Process

Conducting effective legal research requires following a process. This process leads to the authority that controls a legal issue as well as to commentary that may help analyze new and complex legal matters. The outline in Table 1-2 presents the basic research process.

Table 1-2. Overview of the Research Process

1. Determine the jurisdiction controlling the legal issue, if possible, and generate a list of *research terms*.

2. Consult *secondary sources* and practice aids, including treatises, legal encyclopedias, and law review articles, for an overview of the legal area and citations to primary authority.

3. Find controlling *constitutional provisions*, *statutes*, or *administrative rules* and read the relevant sections.

4. Use *case-finding tools*, such as headnotes or full-text searching, to locate any relevant cases. Read the cases.

5. *Update* your legal authorities to ensure they have not been repealed, reversed, modified, or otherwise changed.

6. *End* your research when you have no holes in your analysis and when you begin seeing the same authorities repeatedly.

This basic process should be customized for each research project. Consider whether it is necessary to follow all six steps and, if so, in what order. When researching an unfamiliar area of law, you will need to follow each step of the process in the order indicated. Starting with secondary sources provides both an overview of a legal issue as well as citations to relevant primary authority. With increasing experience in researching legal questions, it may be possible to modify the process. For example, if you know that a situation is controlled by a statute, you may choose to begin with that step. However, be cautious when omitting a step within the research process since failing to find relevant authorities can have severe consequences for both you and your client. If you follow each step and use multiple methods in researching the legal issue, you are more likely to have found all of the relevant authorities.

A. Generating Research Terms

Many legal resources allow you to either browse through an index or search the full text of documents by keyword to locate the legal authority on point. In beginning a successful research project, you will need a comprehensive list of words, terms, and phrases to search. These may be legal terms or common words that describe the client's situation. The items on this list are *research terms.*

Organized brainstorming is the best way to compile a comprehensive list of research terms. Some researchers ask the journalistic questions: Who? What? How? Why? When? Where? Others use a mnemonic device like TARPP, which stands for Things, Actions, Remedies, People, and Places.[15] Whether you use one of these suggestions or develop your own method, generate a broad range of research terms regarding the facts, issues, and desired solutions of your client's situation. Include in the list both specific and general words. Try to think of synonyms and antonyms for each term if you are uncertain which terms may yield the best results. Using a legal dictionary or thesaurus may generate additional terms; some online services suggest alternate terms as you type in your search query.

As an example, assume you are working for a defense attorney recently assigned to a burglary case. Around midnight, your client allegedly used a baseball bat to break a window of a stereo store, where she stole $2,000 worth of equipment. She was charged with aggravated burglary. You have been asked to determine whether there is a good argument for limiting the charge to simple burglary based on the fact that the baseball bat did not constitute a deadly weapon so as to elevate the offense to aggravated burglary. Table 1-3 provides examples of research terms you might use to begin work on this project.

As your research progresses, you will learn new research terms to include in the list and decide to remove others. For example, you may read cases that give you insights into the key words judges tend to use in discussing this topic. Or you may learn a *term of art,* a word or phrase that has special meaning in a particular area of law. These need to be added to the list.

---

15. *See* Steven M. Barkan et al., *Fundamentals of Legal Research* 19 (10th ed. 2015) (explaining "TARP," a similar mnemonic device).

Table 1-3. Generating Research Terms

Journalistic Approach

Who:	Thief, robber, burglar, business owner, property owner
What:	Burglary, aggravated burglary, crime, stolen goods
How:	Breaking and entering, weapon, deadly weapon, trespassing
Why:	Theft, stealing
When:	Midnight
Where:	Store, building, commercial establishment, business, shop

TARPP Approach

Things:	Weapon, deadly weapon, stolen goods
Actions:	Burglary, breaking and entering, trespassing, damages, crime
Remedies:	Burglary, aggravated burglary, incarceration
People:	Thief, robber, burglar, business owner, property owner
Places:	Store, building, commercial establishment, business, shop

B. Researching the Law — Organization of This Text

The remainder of this book explains how to use your research terms to conduct legal research in a variety of sources. The book begins with primary authority because that authority is the goal of research. Chapter 2 addresses the Ohio Constitution, which is the highest legal authority in the state. The other main categories of primary authority are covered in the following chapters: Chapter 3 covers locating and updating statutory law; Chapters 4 and 5 discuss finding and updating case law; Chapter 6 covers court rules and ethical rules; and Chapter 7 discusses administrative law. Chapter 8 covers local law.

Secondary sources are covered in Chapter 9. Although secondary sources are discussed toward the end of the book, they are often the best starting point in researching a legal issue. Legislative history is presented by itself in Chapter 10, since it is neither a traditional secondary source nor a primary source. Chapter 11 discusses research strategies by working through a sample client matter.

While each chapter gives examples of citations to the sources it covers, Chapter 12 explains standard and local citation rules. There are several different types of citation formats. This book uses the format of *The Bluebook: A Uniform System of Citation*[16] and the *ALWD Guide to Legal Citation*[17] for practice documents. Other citation formats are presented in Chapter 12.

Several appendixes offer useful information to the researcher. Appendix A lists topical research guides for Ohio; Appendix B lists commonly used legal terminology and abbreviations; Appendix C lists the law libraries in Ohio; and Appendix D contains a selected bibliography of texts on legal research, writing, and analysis. The general research texts tend to concentrate on federal resources, supplementing this book's brief introduction to those resources.

VI. Selecting Online Sources for Legal Research

There has been an explosion of free and low-cost online sources of legal material, ranging from comprehensive case law available via Google Scholar to federal and state legislative websites that provide access to statutes and administrative codes. Additionally, many state bar memberships offer access to low-cost legal databases like Casemaker and Fastcase to their members. Membership in the Ohio Bar Association includes access to Casemaker, while some local bar associations in Ohio include Fastcase in their member benefits (e.g., Columbus, Cleveland Metropolitan, Dayton, and Toledo).

With these expanding free and low-cost options, it is natural to wonder why attorneys continue to use expensive legal research services like Lexis Advance and WestlawNext. In fact, there are some types of research that can be effectively done on free or lower cost services. This includes accessing primary sources when you have a citation or are looking for a specific document. Additionally, consulting a legal blog post or Wikipedia article for an overview of a legal topic is an acceptable way to begin researching. While it is not enough to stop researching after a Google search or a review of a legal blog post, these resources can contribute to an understanding of a legal issue and offer a starting point for further research.

---

16. *The Bluebook: A Uniform System of Citation* (Columbia Law Review Ass'n et al., eds., 20th ed. 2015).

17. Coleen M. Barger, *ALWD Guide to Legal Citation* (5th ed. 2014).

Federal and state governments are increasingly making primary source material available for free online. Many of these online sources are replacing official print versions and may be certified as the official or authentic version of a legal source. Since online information is susceptible to changes either by hacking (i.e., maliciously destroying or altering) or by benign neglect, it is important to use an official or authentic version when available. An example of authenticated or certified documents can be found on FDsys, a source for federal legal publications such as the United States Code (federal statutes) and the Code of Federal Regulations.[18]

Although the availability and usability of free legal information continues to improve, there are several limitations to free and low-cost sources. They often are not as comprehensive in their coverage as the two premier services, Lexis Advance and WestlawNext. These two premier services also offer invaluable research aids and updating tools that are essential for completing thorough and accurate legal research. Additionally, Lexis Advance and WestlawNext provide access to a wealth of traditional secondary sources, such as treatises, that may greatly facilitate the research process.

Another consideration in using a free or low-cost research tool is the security of the website. Attorneys are obligated to keep certain information private and may decide to keep other information confidential as a matter of strategy. Not all websites or online services guarantee the level of confidentiality needed in some circumstances. When using any online service, it is important to consider the privacy of your activity. This includes the privacy of your device (such as a PC, laptop, or phone), the network (such as your office network or the wireless Internet offered at a coffee shop), and the website itself. While the same information may be available on multiple online systems, each website or service may have different policies about what information is tracked, saved, and shared with third parties. Reviewing terms of service, reviewing privacy policies, and ensuring encrypted data transmission may be necessary when conducting sensitive legal research online.

---

18. For more information on authentication, see the GPO's FDsys Authentication page at www.gpo.gov/authentication/.

Chapter 2

Researching Constitutions

I. Constitutions Generally

Constitutions establish the fundamental structure of a government, assign power to a government's different branches, and guarantee individual rights and liberties. Most governments, including foreign governments, have a basic constitution.

II. The Ohio and U.S. Constitutions

Since its inception in 1803, Ohio has had two constitutions. The original Ohio Constitution of 1802 was replaced by the current constitution, the Ohio Constitution of 1851. Although dating back to the mid-nineteenth century, the current Ohio Constitution has been amended numerous times since 1851.[1] The structure of the Ohio Constitution is similar to the current U.S. Constitution, which dates back to 1787. Like the Ohio Constitution, the U.S. Constitution has been amended many times since its inception.

A. Constitutional Rights

The U.S. Constitution is the supreme law of the United States. In other words, no law may contradict the rights guaranteed by the Constitution. The states, however, may provide greater rights than the federal constitution.[2] As an example, consider a Native American prison guard's refusal to cut his hair,

---

1. For a detailed discussion of Ohio's constitutional history, see Steven H. Steinglass & Gino J. Scarselli, *The Ohio State Constitution* (2011).

2. *Arnold v. Cleveland*, 616 N.E.2d 163, 168 (Ohio 1993).

which violates the grooming policy for guards at Ohio correctional institutions.[3] While his refusal may not be protected by the U.S. Constitution, it is protected by the Ohio Constitution's greater guarantee of religious expression.[4] When researching a constitutional issue in Ohio, it is important to determine whether the Ohio Constitution provides a right identical to or greater than the U.S. Constitution.

B. Unconstitutional Legislation

Both the U.S. Constitution and the Ohio Constitution limit government authority, including the ability of the legislature to enact statutes. Hence, recently enacted statutes may be vulnerable to constitutional challenges. Although the Ohio courts presume legislation to be constitutional,[5] they may find a statute void for violating the procedural requirements of the Ohio Constitution.[6] For example, in 1999 the Ohio Supreme Court determined that a tort reform statute violated the Ohio Constitution's single-subject rule in Section 15(D) of Article II, which prohibits acts that contain more than one subject.[7]

Other procedural limits on the Ohio General Assembly's power involve the uniform operation of laws throughout the state,[8] the application of a statute retroactively,[9] and the ban on incurring debt to provide financial aid to corporations.[10]

C. Other Constitutional Provisions

While the Ohio Constitution mandates the overall structure of the Ohio government (much like the U.S. Constitution does for the federal government), it also contains provisions that are similar in subject matter to federal statutes.

---

3. *See Humphrey v. Lane*, 728 N.E.2d 1039 (Ohio 2000).

4. *Id.* at 1045, 1047.

5. *See Hoover v. Bd. of Cnty. Comm'rs, Franklin Cnty.*, 482 N.E.2d 575, 580 (Ohio 1985).

6. *See State ex rel. Ohio Acad. of Trial Lawyers v. Sheward*, 715 N.E.2d 1062, 1101 (Ohio 1999).

7. *Id.* The single-subject rule attempts to prevent log-rolling, a legislative practice that adds numerous provisions attractive to different small groups of the legislature to ensure a majority of votes in favor of a bill. The Ohio Supreme Court ruled the entire tort reform act unconstitutional as a result of this violation.

8. Ohio Const. art. II, § 26.

9. Ohio Const. art. II, § 28.

10. Ohio Const. art. VIII.

For example, the Ohio Constitution contains detailed requirements for elections,[11] education,[12] corporations,[13] and gaming.[14]

III. Constitutional Amendments

There are several ways the Ohio Constitution may be amended. Amendments to the Ohio Constitution may be proposed by the General Assembly through a joint resolution or by the voters through a ballot initiative.[15] See *The Ohio State Constitution* for a listing of constitutional amendments proposed since 1803.[16] The constitution may also be changed through a constitutional convention. The voters are asked every 20 years to determine if there will be a convention. At any time, the General Assembly may recommend a constitutional convention to the voters. Unlike the Ohio Constitution, the U.S. Constitution may only be amended by Congress or through a constitutional convention.[17]

IV. Researching the Ohio and U.S. Constitutions

To thoroughly research an Ohio or U.S. constitutional issue, follow the steps outlined in Table 2-1.

---

11. Ohio Const. art. V.
12. Ohio Const. art. VI.
13. Ohio Const. art. XIII.
14. Ohio Const. art. XV, §6.
15. A *joint resolution* is a written expression of the General Assembly's opinion passed by both the Senate and House. Recent joint resolutions are available on the General Assembly's website at www.legislature.ohio.gov.
16. *The Ohio State Constitution, supra* note 1. This list is kept up-to-date at http://guides.law.csuohio.edu/ohioconstitution on the "table of proposed amendments" tab.
17. U.S. Const. art. V. An amendment must be ratified by three-quarters of Congress and three-quarters of the state legislatures to pass.

Table 2-1. Outline of Constitutional Law Research

A. Find a secondary source that gives an overview of the legal issue.

B. Find and carefully read the relevant section of the constitution.

C. Find cases that construe or apply the section at issue.

D. Update the constitutional provision to make sure it has not been amended.

E. Research the history of a constitutional provision or constitutional amendment for further background information.

A. Find a Secondary Source for an Overview

It is helpful to start research on a constitutional issue with a secondary source. For an Ohio constitutional issue, *Ohio Jurisprudence 3d*, a legal encyclopedia, provides a good introduction along with citations to applicable cases and statutory sections. Additionally, a law review article may provide a useful discussion of Ohio constitutional provisions. These secondary sources are discussed in Chapter 9.

American Jurisprudence 2d, a general legal encyclopedia, discusses U.S. constitutional provisions. There are numerous other sources dedicated to explaining the U.S. Constitution, such as the *Encyclopedia of the American Constitution*[18] and *Treatise on Constitutional Law*.[19] Also, U.S. constitutional provisions are often discussed in law review articles. Again, refer to Chapter 9 for further coverage of secondary sources.

B. Find the Relevant Text of the Ohio or U.S. Constitution

After consulting a secondary source for an overview, the next step is to actually find and read the specific constitutional provision. The text of the current Ohio Constitution is freely available online from the Ohio General Assembly's website;[20] the U.S. Constitution is freely available from GPO[21] and at Cornell's

---

18. *Encyclopedia of the American Constitution* (Leonard W. Levy et al. eds., 2d ed. 2000).

19. Ronald D. Rotunda & John E. Nowak, *Treatise on Constitutional Law: Substance and Procedure* (5th ed. 2008).

20. The Ohio Legislature, https://www.legislature.ohio.gov.

21. GPO, U.S. Government Publishing Office, http://www.gpo.gov/fdsys/.

Legal Information Institute.[22] However, these versions are often unannotated—meaning that they do not contain cross-references to other resources—and may not be frequently updated. Bloomberg Law provides the text of the Ohio Constitution. It is kept up-to-date, but it is not annotated.

The best place to start is with an annotated version of the constitution. While the Ohio Constitution is not technically a part of the Ohio Revised Code, it is contained in both *Page's Ohio Revised Code Annotated* and *Baldwin's Ohio Revised Code Annotated*.[23] Similarly, the U.S. Constitution is available in West's *United States Code Annotated* and LexisNexis's *United States Code Service*.[24] If you do not have a specific citation to a constitutional provision, use the index to one of the annotated codes available in print or on WestlawNext (Lexis Advance does not have an index); alternatively the full text of the annotated statutory codes may be searched by keyword on either Lexis or Westlaw. In addition to the text of a constitutional provision, the annotated statutory code provides many helpful references, including references to secondary sources, statutes, regulations, and summaries of important cases. Figure 2-1 provides an example of what a constitutional provision looks like online. The constitutional text is followed by the credit section, which indicates the date the section was adopted and any amendments since then.

C. Find Cases That Construe or Apply the Constitution

To locate cases construing or applying the constitution, first examine the cases listed in annotations. For example, in Figure 2-1, the tabs across the top link to cases that interpret the provision (via the "Notes of Decision" and "Citing References" tabs) and other sources that explain or comment on the provision (from the "Context and Analysis" tab). Chapter 3 describes how to find relevant cases using the notes of decision on WestlawNext and the case notes on Lexis Advance. References to cases may also be found in secondary sources, such as *Ohio Jurisprudence 3d* or a law review article. Additionally, searching for cases, discussed in Chapter 5, may be necessary to find all relevant cases on a particular topic, including constitutional provisions.

---

22. Legal Information Institute (LII), www.law.cornell.edu.

23. *Baldwin's Ohio Revised Code Annotated* is available in print and on WestlawNext; *Page's Ohio Revised Code Annotated* is available in print and on Lexis Advance.

24. The *United States Code Annotated* (USCA) is available in print and on WestlawNext; *United States Code Service* (USCS) is available in print and on Lexis Advance.

Figure 2-1. Excerpt from the Constitution of the State of Ohio from WestlawNext

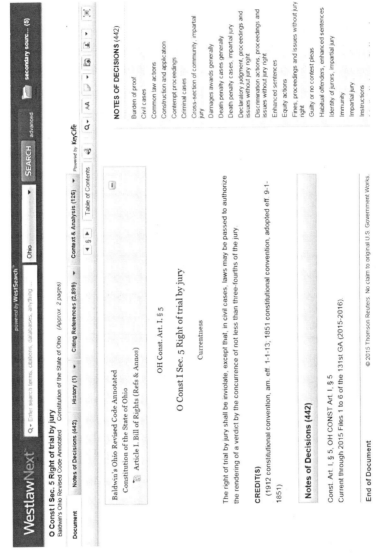

Source: WestlawNext. Reprinted with permission from Thomson Reuters.

D. Update the Constitutional Provision

Because constitutions may be amended, it is important to update constitutional provisions as you would statutes. This process is discussed in Chapter 3, Part IV.E.

E. Research the History of a Constitutional Provision or Constitutional Amendment

To research the history of the passage of a constitutional provision or amendment, start by examining the notes in the annotated statutory code to see if they provide a summary of the provision's history. Next, locate any available debates and proceedings. Debates and recommendations of Ohio constitutional conventions appear in published proceedings and other summaries prepared shortly after each convention.[25] The most comprehensive source for the 1787 U.S. Constitution is *The Documentary History of the Ratification of the Constitution.*[26]

V. Citing Constitutions

When citing the Ohio Constitution or the U.S. Constitution, note that there is no year included except when citing a version of the constitution no longer in effect. Table 2-2 provides examples of references to Article I, Section 7 of the Ohio Constitution that conform to common citation formats.

Table 2-2. Ohio Constitution Citation Example

Citation Method	Example	Source
ALWD Guide	Ohio Const. art. I § 7.	Appendix 1 and Rule 13
Bluebook	Ohio Const. art. I § 7.	Rule 11 and Bluepages B11
*Ohio Manual of Citations**	Ohio Constitution, Article I, Section 7.	Rule 2.1

* The citation rules in the *Ohio Manual of Citations* ("*Ohio Manual*") govern the citation format used for Ohio state opinions. These rules are incorporated into the *Writing Manual: A Guide to Citations, Style and Judicial Opinion* published and kept up-to-date by the Supreme Court of Ohio.

---

25. These resources are available in print at major Ohio law libraries; some are available online on the Ohio Supreme Court's website at www.supremecourtofohio.gov. Lists of the documents related to each constitutional convention appear in the chapter on Ohio's Constitutions in Melanie K. Putnam and Susan M. Schaefgen, *Ohio Legal Research Guide* 19–25 (1997) and in the text and bibliography of *The Ohio State Constitution, supra* note 1.

26. *The Documentary History of the Ratification of the Constitution* (John P. Kaminski et al. eds., 1976).

VI. Additional Resources

A number of helpful resources exist for researching and understanding the Ohio Constitution. Several of the more current resources are listed below.

Melanie K. Putnam & Susan M. Schaefgen, *Ohio's Constitutions*, in *Ohio Legal Research Guide* 1–25 (1997).

Steven H. Steinglass & Gino J. Scarselli, *The Ohio State Constitution* (2011).

Thomas R. Swisher, *Ohio Constitution Handbook* (1990).

Symposium, *The Ohio Constitution—Then and Now: An Examination of the Law and History of the Ohio Constitution on the Occasion of Its Bicentennial*, 51 Clev. St. L. Rev. 333 (2004).

Barbara A. Terzian, *Ohio's Constitutional Conventions and Constitutions*, in 1 *The History of Ohio Law* 40 (Michael Les Benedict & John F. Winkler eds., 2004).

Chapter 3

Researching Statutes

I. Statutes Generally

Much of our law derives from statutes, which are laws passed by a legislative body (e.g., the Ohio General Assembly or the U.S. Congress). Some statutes create duties (e.g., Ohio Revised Code § 2151.421 requires lawyers and others to report suspicions of child abuse).[1] Other statutes create exceptions to these duties (e.g., section 2151.421(a)(3) exempts attorneys from the reporting requirement if reporting their suspicions would violate the attorney-client privilege).[2] Statutes can also prohibit certain behaviors and impose punishments.

A legal issue may involve either state or federal statutes or perhaps both, so an Ohio practitioner must be comfortable with both Ohio and federal statutory research. The following sections provide an overview of the statutory research process, covering how statutes are published, researched, and updated.

II. Ohio Statutes

Both state and federal statutes appear in two basic formats: chronologically in session laws and by subject in statutory codes. Most often, you will be searching for statutes on a specific subject, so a codified collection of statutes—a statutory code—is the best place to start. However, session laws are valuable in researching changes to statutory language and its legislative history. This section discusses the various sources for Ohio statutes, while the next section addresses sources for federal statutes.

---

1. Ohio Rev. Code Ann. § 2151.421 (LexisNexis 2011).
2. *Id.* at § 2151.421(a)(3).

A. Session Laws

At the end of each two-year session of the Ohio General Assembly, the statutes enacted during that session are published chronologically as session laws in the *Laws of Ohio*. While the session laws in the *Laws of Ohio* are the official source of Ohio statutes, its publication lags several years. Several commercial publications provide quicker access to new Ohio statutes. Known as "advanced legislative services," *Baldwin's Ohio Legislative Service* (available in print and on WestlawNext) and *Page's Bulletin* (available in print and on Lexis Advance) both promptly publish new laws. Also, new laws from 1997 to present are available through the Ohio General Assembly's website.[3] Session laws from 1788, including the Territory of Ohio, are available on HeinOnline.[4]

B. Statutory Codes

The Ohio Revised Code arranges Ohio's statutes into 33 titles.[5] For example, Title 11 covers financial institutions, and Title 29 covers crimes and criminal procedure. Each title is further divided into chapters, and each chapter into sections. Table 3-1 provides an example of the breakdown of chapters within a title.

Table 3-1. Chapters in Title 43, Liquors

Chapter 4301.	Liquor Control Law
Chapter 4303.	Liquor Permits
Chapter 4305.	Tax on Bulk Sales of Beer
Chapter 4307.	Tax on Bottled Beverages
Chapter 4309.	Brewers' Wort and Malt Tax [Repealed]
Chapter 4311.	Wines — Adulteration; Misbranding [Repealed]
Chapter 4313.	Transfer of Enterprise Acquisition Project to JobsOhio
Chapter 4399.	Prohibitory Provisions and Crimes

---

3. The address is https://www.legislature.ohio.gov.

4. HeinOnline is a subscription database (similar to Lexis and Westlaw) and is available at heinonline.org. If you are using HeinOnline that your organization (e.g., your school's library or your firm) has paid for, access the database through your organization's webpage.

5. Although most statutes are codified and placed into the Ohio Revised Code, statutes deemed only temporary are not codified and are referred to as "uncodified law."

All titles in the Ohio Revised Code are odd-numbered except Title 58, which became the first even-numbered title in 2007.

Citations to the Ohio Revised Code include the chapter and section number: for Ohio Rev. Code § 4301.62, the chapter number is 4301, and the section number is 62.

Although there is no official government version of the Ohio Revised Code, there is a free version available online.[6] However, this version lacks the valuable supplemental material available in the annotated statutory codes discussed below. Similarly, Bloomberg Law provides the Ohio Revised Code, which can be searched by table of contents or with full-text queries. The Bloomberg version does not provide annotations, so you would have to run additional searches to find related secondary sources, cases, rules, and other related documents.

C. Annotated Statutory Codes

The two annotated versions of Ohio's statutory code are *Page's Ohio Revised Code Annotated* (published by LexisNexis and available on Lexis Advance) and *Baldwin's Ohio Revised Code Annotated* (published by West and available on WestlawNext). Along with the text of each code section, the annotations contain references to secondary sources, other relevant primary authority (such as constitutional provisions and regulations), and summaries of important cases. Figure 3-1 is an excerpt of an Ohio code section with annotations labeled.

Although a statutory code section might itself be quite short, often the accompanying annotations span multiple pages. These annotations contain valuable information worth examining.

III. Federal Statutes

Although the names of the respective Ohio and federal statutory publications are different, the basic system of statutory publication is quite similar and serves the same purpose to the legal researcher.

---

6. The online version, with information about its currency, is available at http://codes.ohio.gov.

Figure 3-1. Excerpt from *Baldwin's Ohio Revised Code Annotated*

§ 2921.11. Perjury

(A) No person, in any official proceeding, shall knowingly make a false statement under oath or affirmation, or knowingly swear or affirm the truth of a false statement previously made, when either statement is material.

* * *

(F) Whoever violates this section is guilty of perjury, a felony of the third degree.

This is the text of the statute.

(1972 H 511, eff. 1-1-74)

HISTORICAL AND STATUTORY NOTES

Ed. Note: 2921.11 contains provisions analogous to former 2917.25, 2917.34, 2945.62, and 4709.21, repealed by 1972 H 511, eff. 1-1-74.

* * *

The history note indicates when this section was enacted and if it has been amended. It was enacted in 1972 by House Bill 511, became effective on January 1, 1974, and was similar to former sections, and has not been amended since.

CROSS REFERENCES

Affidavits on facts relating to title, 5301.252

Allegations in perjury indictment, 2941.18

Transactional immunity, exceptions, 2945.44

LIBRARY REFERENCES

Perjury 1 to 16.

C.J.S. Perjury §§ 2 to 3, 5 to 34, 53 to 56.

The references provide starting points for further research, including other code sections, topic and key numbers, and secondary sources.

RESEARCH REFERENCES

Encyclopedias

OH Jur. 3d Criminal Law § 1414, Generally; Providing False Information or Evidence.

OH Jur. 3d Criminal Law § 1418, Definitions.

OH Jur. 3d Criminal Law § 1420, Materiality of Statement as Element of Offense.

NOTES OF DECISIONS

Action for damages for perjury 6

Affidavit in forma pauperis 4

Constitutional issues 1

Culpable mental state 2

Evidence 5

Official proceeding 3

Case annotations (notes of decisions) provide summaries of cases that interpret or apply the statute. If there are cases on several topics, an outline lists the topics covered. Examples of these annotations are below.

1. Constitutional issues

This is a case annotation.

Plaintiffs failed to establish error based on trial court's alleged failure to follow proper procedure at preliminary hearing in perjury action brought against police officer, where regularity of hearing would be presumed, given that Court of Appeal did not have transcript of hearing, and plaintiffs failed to show prejudice from trial court's alleged failure to follow proper procedure, as perjury claim was properly dismissed. Sherlock v. Myers (Ohio App. 9 Dist., Summit, 09-29-2004) No. 22071, 2004-Ohio-5178, 2004 WL 2244102, Unreported. Appeal And Error 907(2); Appeal And Error 1043(1)

A. Session Laws

Similar to state statutes, federal statutes (called public laws) are published both as session laws and also in a codified form.[7] At the end of a session of the U.S. Congress, the laws enacted during that session are published in the *Statutes at Large*, the official publication of federal statutes. The *Statutes at Large* is available in print and online through FDsys[8] (from the 108th Congress), and HeinOnline (from the 1st Congress). Public laws are also available through the Library of Congress's Congress.gov site. A commercial publication of federal session laws, the *United States Code Congressional & Administrative News* (USCCAN), also provides timely access to federal session laws. USCCAN is available on WestlawNext and in print.

B. Statutory Codes

As with Ohio statutes, federal statutes are also codified so that they are more easily searched by subject. Although Ohio does not have an official version of its statutory code, there is an official version of the federal statutory code. Called the *United States Code* (USC), it arranges the federal statutes into 54 titles.[9] The USC is published in print; it is also available online from several sources including the U.S. House of Representatives,[10] FDsys, Bloomberg, HeinOnline, and Cornell's Legal Information Institute.[11] The USC contains a modest index and several useful tables, such as a popular names table listing federal statutes by popular name (e.g., the Americans with Disabilities Act, the USA Patriot Act) and their corresponding location within the statutory

---

7. Most laws passed by the U.S. Congress are public laws, meaning laws that apply to the general public. However, there are a few private laws as well, which apply only to specific individuals. Private laws often address issues involving individual property, government compensation, or immigration status. For an example of private laws, visit www.gpo.gov/fdsys/ and follow the link to "Public and Private Laws."

8. FDsys is a website maintained by the Government Publishing Office (GPO) at www.gpo.gov/fdsys/.

9. Within the USC, some titles are referred to as positive law titles. Positive law titles have been enacted by Congress, so those positive law titles constitute legal evidence of the law. Non-positive law titles, those titles that have not been enacted into law by Congress, only constitute prima facie evidence of the law. For more information on this distinction and a list of positive law titles, visit http://uscode.house.gov/codification/legislation.shtml.

10. The address is http://uscode.house.gov.

11. The Legal Information Institute is a free resource that has a history of providing accurate and current legal information. It is available at www.law.cornell.edu/uscode.

code. However, the utility of this version of the USC as a research tool is very limited since it is updated infrequently and is not annotated.

C. Annotated Statutory Codes

The two annotated versions of the USC prove more useful for research: the *United States Code Annotated* (USCA), available in print and on WestlawNext, and the *United States Code Service* (USCS), available in print and on Lexis Advance. Similar to the annotated versions of the Ohio Revised Code, the USCA and USCS contain statutes supplemented with references to related resources such as cases, federal regulations, law review articles, treatises, and lists of amendments to each code section. The USCA and USCS also offer more in-depth indexes to the code and helpful tables. The index to the USCA is available on WestlawNext in addition to being available in print. The index to USCS is available only in print, not on Lexis Advance.

IV. Statutory Research Process

Table 3-2 and the following section outline the basic process for researching a statutory issue.

Table 3-2. Overview of the Ohio Statutory Research Process

1. Generate a list of research terms.

2. Consult secondary sources such as treatises, legal encyclopedias, and law review articles for an overview of the legal area and citations to primary authority.

3. Find and read the controlling statutory provision by using an index to the annotated statutory code or searching the full text of the code.

4. Use the annotations or other case finding tools to locate and read any relevant cases.

5. Update the statutory provision to ensure it has not been amended or ruled unconstitutional.

A. Develop a List of Research Terms

The first step in researching a statutory issue is to develop a list of research terms. These are words that are likely to be in the statutory language or in an index. Use one of the brainstorming methods explained in Chapter 1, or design a brainstorming approach that works for you.

B. Consult Secondary Sources for an Overview and Citations to Primary Authority

Next, review the available secondary sources for an overview of the legal area, to determine if the issue is a state or federal issue and if it is governed by statutory law. If the legal area is new to you, consider using a legal encyclopedia such as *American Jurisprudence 2d* or *Ohio Jurisprudence 3d* to answer the important initial questions and to obtain citations to primary sources, such as statutory code sections and cases.

C. Find and Read the Statutory Language

If you have found a citation to a relevant statute through related research or in a secondary source, go directly to the statutory code section. If not, use one of the following techniques to find relevant statutory sections: (1) use the index to the annotated statutory code, (2) browse the table of contents, or (3) do a full-text search.

Starting with the statutory index is often more efficient than full-text searching. All annotated statutory codes in print have indexes; WestlawNext also provides indexes to state and federal statutory codes.[12] Each print statutory code has a general index covering the entire code and shorter indexes at the end of each title. If you are not certain that your code section is in a particular title, use the general index. If using an index is an unfamiliar experience, remember to be both patient and flexible. If your research terms do not appear in the index, think of possible synonyms or antonyms. Note that cross-references will direct you to the proper terminology. For example, the entry for "airplane" redirects to "aircraft and aviation."

Additionally, browsing the table of contents (available in print and on Lexis Advance and WestlawNext) allows you to see the structure of the code and to view statutory sections in context. Because codes are arranged by subject area, neighboring sections often contain definitional sections, exceptions, penalties, and other related sections. Table 3-3 lists common statutory sections relating to bank offenses, showing the relationship between neighboring sections.

---

12. Currently, the Lexis Advance online versions of *Page's Ohio Revised Code Annotated* and the *United States Code Service* do not have an index.

Table 3-3. Sections of Chapter 1101, Banks — Offenses

1101.01 Definitions.

1101.02 Purpose.

1101.03 Applicability of provisions.

1101.10 Public records.

1101.15 Use of terms, serving as trustee or fiduciary.

1101.16 Requirements for accepting deposits.

1101.99 Penalties.

If using the statutory code index or browsing the table of contents proves ineffective, full-text searching in an online statutory database is another way to locate relevant statutes. Combine relevant research terms to build a comprehensive search of the statutes in an online database. See Chapter 5, Part II for guidance on full-text searching.

D. Find Cases that Interpret or Apply the Statute

After locating an applicable statutory section, the next step is to find cases applying the statute. To predict how a court is likely to apply the statute to a particular set of facts, it is useful to know how courts have done so in the past. A court may also rule parts of the statute unconstitutional or find application of the statute to a certain situation unconstitutional. Moreover, what appears to be simple or clear language of a statute may not be.

The easiest way to find relevant cases is to use the case annotations in the applicable annotated statutory codes, such as *Baldwin's Ohio Revised Code* or *United States Code Annotated*, either in print or online. The case annotations list cases that have applied that statutory code section. However, you must not rely on these case summaries alone as they do not provide the full context of the case and occasionally contain incomplete or inaccurate information. Instead, use the citation at the end of the summary to locate and examine the full case.

E. Updating Statutes

Updating is an essential step in legal research. Updating statutory codes involves checking for new and amending statutes and for cases that may have invalidated the statute. If using a print code, check the following for new or amending statutory language:

- Pocket parts and supplements located at the back of the volumes and on the shelves.
- Advance legislative services such as *Baldwin's Ohio Legislative Service* or *Page's Bulletin* (which cover new Ohio laws) or USCCAN (which covers new federal laws).

If researching online, WestlawNext, Lexis Advance, and other databases likely provide the current text, but you should check the date by clicking the "i" icon or "Currency" link.

You also need to update with citators, which is the fifth step in the research process. To do so, check the following:

- If using WestlawNext, KeyCite the statutory code section to identify statutory amendments or pending legislation. KeyCite also includes cases citing the statutory code in addition to secondary sources.
- If using Lexis Advance, keep in mind that Shepard's provides the same information for statutes as does KeyCite. Lexis Advance gives a link to new statutes not yet included in the statutory code and gives you an alert when a pending bill would affect the code section. Shepardizing a statute will provide a list of citing cases and secondary sources.

Because WestlawNext and Lexis Advance provide more current information than print sources, complete updating requires use of one of those services even if you are primarily conducting statutory research in print. However, keep in mind that there might be a lag between the time a law is generated and when WestlawNext and Lexis Advance are updated with that new information.

V. Other Research Tools

In addition to annotated statutory codes, several other tools may assist with research of statutes based on uniform laws, with statutory research across jurisdictions, and with historical statutory research. These resources include uniform laws, model acts, and statutory surveys.

A. Uniform Laws and Model Acts

Uniform laws and model acts are proposed statutory schemes. The authors of *uniform laws* seek uniformity among states to facilitate interstate commerce;

the National Conference of Commissioners on Uniform State Laws (NCCUSL) drafts most of the existing uniform laws. The Uniform Commercial Code is the most successful uniform law, having been adopted by all states. As opposed to uniform laws, the main goal of *model acts* lies in legal reform rather than uniformity; the Model Penal Code is a well-known example of a model act drafted by the American Law Institute. Uniform laws and model acts are not the law in a given jurisdiction unless adopted by that jurisdiction.

Uniform Laws Annotated (ULA), published by West and also available on WestlawNext, provides a good starting place for researching uniform laws and some model acts. For each law, ULA lists the jurisdictions that have adopted it and its location within the respective jurisdictions' statutory codes. It also notes how each jurisdiction has modified or changed the original text of the uniform law. The texts of many uniform laws are also freely available online at the National Law Conference website[13] and through Cornell's Legal Information Institute.[14]

B. Statutory Surveys

Statutory surveys offer invaluable research assistance when you are researching statutory issues in multiple jurisdictions. For specific issues such as medical records, right to die, or stalking laws, a statutory survey lists the corresponding state statutory code sections. The Subject Compilation of State Laws, an index of state statutory surveys, is available on HeinOnline. Statutory, as well as regulatory, surveys are also available on WestlawNext and Lexis Advance. The National Center for State Legislatures provides free access to its collection of state surveys on its website.[15]

C. Archived Codes

Sometimes research requires finding a prior version of a statute. For example, a criminal appeal may focus on the text of a statute that has been amended since the crime occurred. While the code contains the text of only the current version of the law, it does indicate when the section was amended and provides citations to the prior versions of the section in the history note. This note appears after the statutory language and before the annotations. Refer to Figure 3-2 for an example of a history note. Additionally, both Lexis Advance and

---

13. The address is http://www.uniformlawcommission.com.
14. The LII website is at www.law.cornell.edu.
15. NCSL's collection of state surveys is available at http://www.ncsl.org; click on "Bill Information Service" at the bottom of the page.

WestlawNext have archives of prior versions of the code. Also, many academic law libraries retain superseded codes, either in print or microform.

VI. Citing Statutes

When citing a statutory code section, the format is the same in the *ALWD Guide* and the *Bluebook*, but significantly different in the *Ohio Manual of Citations*. Notably, the *Ohio Manual of Citations* format omits the publication date of the statutory code and the section symbol (§) required by the *ALWD Guide* and the *Bluebook*.

Table 3-4 puts §2151.421 of *Baldwin's Ohio Revised Code Annotated* in each of the common citation formats. Note that the only difference in a citation to *Page's Ohio Revised Code Annotated* would be the publisher in the parenthetical.

Table 3-4. Ohio Statute Citation Example

Citation Method	Example	Source
ALWD Guide	Ohio Rev. Code Ann. §2151.421 (West Supp. 2014).	Rule 14.4, Appendix 1
Bluebook	Ohio Rev. Code Ann. §2151.421 (West Supp. 2014).	Rule 12, Table T1, and Bluepages B12.1.2
Ohio Manual of Citations	R.C. 2151.421.	Rule 3.1

Table 3-5 shows §206 of Title 29 of the USC, which is the federal minimum wage law, in the two citation formats.

Table 3-5. Federal Statute Citation Example

Citation Method	Example	Source
ALWD Guide	29 U.S.C. § 206 (2012).	Rule 14
Bluebook	29 U.S.C. § 206 (2012).	Rule 12, Table T1, and Bluepages B12.1.1
Ohio Manual of Citations	29 U.S.C. 206.	Rule 3.3

Chapter 4

Understanding Cases

I. Cases and Court Reporters Generally

A court writes a judicial opinion, or a case, to explain its decision in a particular dispute. Case law was traditionally published in print reporters but is now increasingly available from free Internet sources and from commercial online databases, like Bloomberg Law, Lexis Advance, and WestlawNext. Although most case law research is conducted online, an understanding of the traditional publication of cases is necessary for effective case law research and case citation.

Many cases are published chronologically in different types of reporters. Some reporters include only cases decided by a particular court. For example, *Ohio State Reports* contains opinions decided by the Ohio Supreme Court. Other reporters contain cases from courts within a specific geographic region. The *North Eastern Reporter*, a regional reporter, publishes Ohio's appellate cases along with cases from nearby states. Reporters may also publish cases only on a specific subject matter, such as education law, bankruptcy, or media law. Hence, a single case can appear in multiple reporters.

Some reporters are deemed "official." Official reporters are generally published or adopted by the government. However, there are many "unofficial" commercial reporters, most of which are published by West, which provide more timely access to cases and supplemental research aids. Not all state jurisdictions publish an official reporter, instead relying on West's commercial reporters for the print publication of their state cases. Refer to Table T1 of the *Bluebook* and Appendix 1 of the *ALWD Guide* for a listing of the respective reporters covering each jurisdiction. In citing to a case, citation rules often prefer a given reporter, such as the official reporter or the commercial, regional reporter. Check the controlling citation rules to decide which reporter, if any, to include in a citation.

II. Publication of Ohio Cases

A *slip opinion* is the initial opinion issued by the court. A slip opinion is generally available from the court that decided the case, often on its website. Slip opinions do not contain editorial enhancements normally added by publishers, so they are of limited value in legal research. There are both official and unofficial publishers of Ohio cases.

A. Official Publication

Official publication of Ohio Cases occurs online instead of in print.[1] As of July 1, 2012, Ohio discontinued official publication in print and substituted with official publication online. The Supreme Court designated its website publication as the *Ohio Official Reports*.[2] Court rules require all Supreme Court, Courts of Appeals, and Court of Claims opinions to be published on the Supreme Court website.[3] The Court of Claims, however, is the only Ohio trial court with officially reported opinions; no official reporter (either in print or online) exists for other Ohio trial court opinions. Significantly, the new rules provide for permanent public access—all opinions posted to the Supreme Court website "shall be permanently available to the public without charge."[4]

Because Ohio's online resources were not official before July 1, 2012, it is important to understand the pre-2012 official print reporters as well. Before moving to official non-print publication,[5] Ohio had three official print reporters: *Ohio State Reports*, *Ohio Appellate Reports*, and *Ohio Miscellaneous Reports*. Until 1991, these three reporters were published jointly in one volume

---

1. *See Reporter of Decisions—Opinions and Announcements*, The Supreme Court of Ohio, www.sconet.state.oh.us/ROD/docs/.

2. The Ohio Supreme Court announced the new *Ohio Official Reports* in its Supreme Court Rules for Reporting of Opinions ("Rep. O.R."). *See* Rep. O.R. 3.2, *available at* Supreme Court of Ohio, Ohio Rules of Court, www.sconet.state.oh.us/LegalResources/Rules/reporting/Report.pdf.

3. *See id.* at 2.1 and 3.3.

4. *Id.* at 4.3.

5. The Ohio Supreme Court refers to opinions published electronically as non-print published, a term that more accurately describes opinions that are published electronically. Often opinions reported online but not in print are referred to as "unpublished" or "unreported." Because the cases in question are published electronically, unpublished is a misnomer, which explains the Ohio Supreme Court's choice to use non-print published instead of unpublished or unreported.

called the *Ohio Official Reports* (abbreviated "O.O."). The Ohio Supreme Court resurrected the name for the Supreme Court's website publication, which, as noted above, now is designated *Ohio Official Reports.*

Ohio State Reports (abbreviated "Ohio St.") contains only opinions of the Ohio Supreme Court. *Ohio State Reports* is the only one of the three Ohio reporters still in print, but it is no longer the "official" publication. While *Ohio State Reports* is still published, the other two print reporters, *Ohio Appellate Reports* and *Ohio Miscellaneous Reports*, are no longer published. Until July 1, 2012, *Ohio Appellate Reports* (abbreviated "Ohio App.") published in print selected opinions of Ohio's Courts of Appeals. *Ohio Miscellaneous Reports* (abbreviated "Ohio Misc.") published in print a small number of Ohio trial court opinions.

B. Print Published and Non-Print Published Distinction

Like many jurisdictions, Ohio once distinguished between print published (also called reported or published) and non-print published (also called unreported or unpublished) opinions from Ohio's Courts of Appeals. Print published opinions were deemed binding precedent, while non-print published opinions were not binding. On May 1, 2002, however, the Supreme Court amended its Rules for Reporting of Opinions to dispense with the distinction between print published and non-print published opinions for Court of Appeals opinions. Since this amendment, court rules have provided that decisions of the intermediate appellate courts "may be cited as legal authority and weighted as deemed appropriate by the courts without regard to whether the opinion was published or in what form it was published."[6] This distinction remains important when citing older opinions. To decide whether a non-print published case is binding depends on the date it was decided. If a non-print published case was decided before May 1, 2002, it can be cited as only persuasive authority. Accordingly, if a lawyer relies upon a non-print published opinion decided before May 1, 2002, the rules suggest that the court may consider that opinion merely persuasive and not binding. The rules never made this distinction for trial court opinions, probably because so few trial court opinions were print published, even when the reporter for trial court decisions still existed.

---

6. Rep. O.R. 3.4. The previous version of the Rules for Reporting of Opinions used similar language. The predecessor rules provided that non-print published opinions of the courts of appeals were persuasive and not controlling.

C. Unofficial Print Publication

Ohio cases may also be found in the *North Eastern Reporter* (abbreviated "N.E."), one of West's regional reporters. The *North Eastern Reporter* contains cases from the appellate courts of Ohio, Illinois, Indiana, Massachusetts, and New York. West also publishes other state appellate cases in its other regional reporters: *Atlantic Reporter*, *North Western Reporter*, *Pacific Reporter*, *South Eastern Reporter*, *South Western Reporter*, and *Southern Reporter*. While the text of the court's opinion is the same in the official and unofficial regional reporters, the appearance, pagination, and editorial additions may be different. Table 4-1 lists which states appear in the respective regional reporters.

Table 4-1. State Cases Included in Regional Reporters

Atlantic Reporter	Connecticut, Delaware, District of Columbia, Maine, Maryland, New Hampshire, New Jersey, Pennsylvania, Rhode Island, and Vermont
North Eastern Reporter	Illinois, Indiana, Massachusetts, New York, and Ohio
North Western Reporter	Iowa, Michigan, Minnesota, Nebraska, North Dakota, South Dakota, and Wisconsin
South Eastern Reporter	Georgia, North Carolina, South Carolina, Virginia, and West Virginia
South Western Reporter	Arkansas, Kentucky, Missouri, Tennessee, and Texas
Southern Reporter	Alabama, Florida, Louisiana, and Mississippi
Pacific Reporter	Alaska, Arizona, California, Colorado, Hawaii, Idaho, Kansas, Montana, Nevada, New Mexico, Oklahoma, Oregon, Utah, Washington, and Wyoming

The assignment of states into the respective regional reporters was determined by West and does not correlate with the composition of the federal circuits. Ohio is in the federal Sixth Circuit, which includes Michigan, Ohio, Kentucky, and Tennessee, yet only Ohio's state cases appear in the *North Eastern Reporter*.

III. Reporters for Federal Cases

There are numerous reporters dedicated to reporting just federal cases. Table 4-2 lists the main federal case reporters.

Table 4-2. Reporters for Federal Court Cases

U.S. Supreme Court	*United States Reports* (official)
	Supreme Court Reporter
	United States Supreme Court Reports, Lawyers' Edition
U.S. Courts of Appeals	*Federal Reporter*
	Federal Appendix
U.S. District Courts	*Federal Supplement*

All opinions of the United States Supreme Court are reported in:

- the *United States Reports* (abbreviated "U.S."), which is the official reporter,
- the *Supreme Court Reporter* (abbreviated "S. Ct."), published by West,
- the *United States Supreme Court Reports, Lawyers' Edition* (abbreviated "L. Ed."), published by LexisNexis, and
- the *United States Law Week*, published by Bloomberg BNA (Bureau of National Affairs).

When possible, cite to the *United States Reports* because it is the official reporter. However, given the lag in its publication, it may be necessary to cite one of the commercial reporters.

Selected cases decided by the federal intermediate appellate courts, called United States Circuit Courts or the Courts of Appeals, are published in the *Federal Reporter*. The abbreviations for these reporters are F., F.2d, and F.3d. Cases not selected for print publication in the *Federal Reporter* may be printed in the *Federal Appendix*.[7] Additionally, each of the federal Courts of Appeals provides free access to recent cases from its respective website.[8]

Selected decisions from the United States District Courts, the federal trial courts, are reported in the *Federal Supplement*. The abbreviations for these re-

---

7. The precedential value of these "unpublished" cases varies by circuit. The Sixth Circuit permits citation of unpublished opinions. When filing a document with a court within the Sixth Circuit, attach copies of any unpublished cases unless the opinion is available in a publically accessible database. *See* 6th Cir. R. 32.1(b). Be sure to review local court rules before relying on a circuit court case that is not published in the *Federal Reporter*.

8. Go to www.uscourts.gov for links to each website. However, coverage on these websites varies. Some include only published cases, while others include all cases. Some post cases and then remove them, while others keep all cases available.

porters are F. Supp. and F. Supp. 2d. FDsys collects selected federal court opinions, including courts in the Sixth Circuit.[9] Some opinions are also available at Cornell's Legal Information Institute website.[10]

IV. Topical Reporters

Some reporters publish cases on a particular topic, rather than choosing to publish cases from a particular court or region. For example, *West's Education Law Reporter* includes selected state and federal cases that analyze legal issues in education. Similarly, *Bankruptcy Reporter* includes cases from federal courts on that topic.

One of the main publishers of topical reporters is Bloomberg BNA, which is a private company, not a government agency. Bloomberg BNA publishes a wide range of topical reporters, from the *Family Law Reporter*, to the *Daily Tax Report*, to the *Media Law Reporter*. When working in a specialized area of law, check if there is a Bloomberg BNA reporter covering your practice area since they are useful tools for keeping up-to-date with legal developments.

V. Online Commercial Sources for Cases

A *slip opinion* is issued by the court without the editorial enhancements normally added by the publisher. A slip opinion is generally available from the court that decided the case. Increasingly, courts are making their slip opinions available online from their respective websites. The Supreme Court of Ohio provides timely access to its decisions and those of lower Ohio courts on its website.[11] The U.S. Supreme Court also posts its opinions on its website.[12] Check Cornell's Legal Information Institute[13] or FindLaw[14] for links to other free sources of cases.

---

9. FDsys contains opinions for the Sixth Circuit back to 2004. To search or browse these opinions, visit FDsys.gov and select "United States Courts Opinions" under "Browse."

10. *See* Legal Information Institute (LII), Cornell University Law School, www.law.cornell.edu/.

11. *See* The Supreme Court of Ohio, *supra* note 1.

12. *See* Supreme Court of the United States, www.supremecourt.gov/.

13. *See* Legal Information Institute, *supra* note 10.

14. *See* FindLaw, www.findlaw.com/. FindLaw is a website maintained by Thomson Reuters.

Although there are many free sources for cases, many practitioners rely on commercial services to search for case law (mainly Lexis Advance and West-lawNext, with a growing number also using Bloomberg Law). The reasons for this preference for commercial services include comprehensiveness, centralization, search features, and citators:

- Both Lexis Advance and WestlawNext boast comprehensive collections of case law that go back to the 1800s, while most free sources only cover recent years. Bloomberg Law also provides an extensive collection of federal and state court opinions, but as of this writing, Bloomberg Law's opinions do not go back as far as those on Lexis Advance and WestlawNext.

- Additionally, Bloomberg Law, Lexis Advance, and WestlawNext allow for searching different combinations of case law databases through one centralized interface. It is possible to search Ohio cases and federal cases, just Ohio cases, just Sixth Circuit cases, or just federal cases.

- Bloomberg Law, Lexis Advance, and WestlawNext offer sophisticated search features, including the ability to search by headnotes (limited in Bloomberg Law) and fields and to use Boolean and proximity operators.

- Bloomberg Law, Lexis Advance, and WestlawNext also offer citators, which are essential in checking the status of a case.

See Chapter 5 for a discussion on the various approaches to finding cases; that discussion will explain many concepts mentioned in the bullet points above.

VI. Features of a Case

A court opinion published in a print reporter or commercial service typically contains supplemental information intended to aid researchers in learning about the case, locating relevant parts of the case, and finding similar cases. Some of these research aids are gleaned from the court's opinion, while others are written by the publisher's or service's editorial staff. The following discussion explains the information and enhancements included in *Ohio State Reports*. Most cases, whether found in a print reporter or online, will include most of these items, though perhaps in a different order.

Note that the excerpt in Figure 4-1 is from a case published by the state, not by West, so editorial enhancements are slightly different from those in *North Eastern Reporter* or those available online.

Parties and Procedural Designations. Each case begins with the caption, which identifies the parties of the case and indicates their procedural designa-

Figure 4-1. Excerpt of Ohio Case from *Ohio State Reports*

1 Ohio St. 3d   STATE v. FANNING   19
                                 Opinion, per Reilly, J

Parties and Procedural Designation →   THE STATE OF OHIO, APPELLEE, V. FANNING, APPELLANT.

[Cite as State v. Fanning (1982), 1 Ohio St. 3d 19.]

Criminal law—Jury instructions—Defendant's failure to testify—Requested instruction mandatory—Motions to suppress in-court identification and to dismiss for lack of speedy trial—Properly overruled, when.

O.Jur 3d Criminal Law § 1015.

Syllabus → 1. A trial judge has the constitutional obligation, upon proper request, to minimize the danger that the jury will give evidentiary weight to a defendant's failure to testify. Upon proper request, defendant has a right, under the privilege against compulsory self-incrimination guaranteed by the Fifth Amendment, to have the judge instruct the jury that the defendant's failure to testify cannot be considered for any purpose. The trial court has a mandatory constitutional duty to give such a requested instruction. (State v. Nelson, 36 Ohio St. 2d 79 [65 O.O.2d 222] paragraph three of the syllabus, overruled.)

* * *

Docket Number and Date of Decision →   (No. 81.679—Decided July 14, 1982.)

APPEAL from the Court of Appeals for Hamilton County.

Defendant-appellant, Irving Fanning, was indicted on one count of aggravated robbery (R.C. 2911.01). He allegedly entered the Hi-Val Service Station and went to the manager's office with an employee. The manager, Robert Carr, opened his office door. Appellant pointed a gun at him, then tied him and the employee and fled with $2800. Police were called, and Carr gave them a description of his assailant. Subsequently, appellant was arrested based on eyewitness identification made by Carr.

Appellant filed a motion to suppress the in-court identification and after a hearing the motion was overruled.... The Court of Appeals affirmed, and the cause is now before this court pursuant to the allowance of a motion for leave to appeal.

Mr. Simon L. Leis, Jr., prosecuting attorney. Mr. Leonard Kirschner and Mr. James Applegate, for appellee.

Opinion   Ms. Alma Yaros, for appellant.

→ REILLY, Judge. Appellant advances three propositions of law:

* * *

3. "A defendant in a state criminal trial has the right under the privilege against compulsory self-incrimination protected by the Fifth Amendment as made applicable to the states by the Fourteenth Amendment, upon request, to have the judge instruct the jury that the fact that the defendant did not testify cannot be considered for any purpose, the state trial judge having the constitutional obligation, upon proper request, to minimize the danger that the jury will give evidentiary weight to a defendant's failure to testify."

* * *

Consequently, this court must overrule the determination in State v. Nelson (1973), 36 Ohio St.2d 79 [65 O.O.2d 222], paragraph three of the syllabus, wherein it was held that it was discretionary with the trial judge whether to instruct the jury on the defendant's rights to elect not to testify. Since appellant's case was pending on appeal at the time of the Carter decision, this court must apply the rule as announced in Carter. Linkletter v. Walker (1965), 381 U.S. 618, 639.

* * *

For the foregoing reasons, the judgment of the Court of Appeals is affirmed.

Disposition →   *Judgment affirmed.*

W. BROWN, Acting C. J., and SWEENEY, LOCHER, HOLMES, C. BROWN and KRU-PANSKY, JJ., concur.

REILLY, J., of the Tenth Appellate District, sitting for CELEBREZZE, C. J.

tions. In general, the party seeking appellate review is called the appellant and the opposing party is the appellee.[15]

Library References. Some reporters give cross-references to the relevant sections of a legal encyclopedia such as *Ohio Jurisprudence*. The legal encyclopedia coverage often provides valuable background information and references to additional, relevant primary authority such as cases and statutes.

Syllabus. The syllabus consists of a short summary of the case. Skimming the syllabus during research can quickly tell you whether a case is relevant to your project. In an Ohio Supreme Court opinion, the syllabus is written by the court.[16] In cases published before May 1, 2002, only the syllabus of an Ohio Supreme Court opinion stated the controlling law. Current court rules clarify that both the text of the case and the syllabus state the law.[17]

Docket Number. Courts assign each case a unique number, called a docket number. Docket numbers are helpful in locating parties' briefs, court orders, or other documents related to the case. These court documents may be available only from the court, which may require the docket number to retrieve them.[18]

Date. The date indicates the date the case was decided. This is the date you will use in your citation. Sometimes, the date that the case was argued will also appear.

Parallel Cites. As explained earlier, cases are often published in multiple reporters or online databases. The text of an opinion reported at parallel cites is identical, although some of the editorial enhancements may be different.

Headnotes. A headnote is a sentence or short paragraph that sets out a single point of law in a case. Most cases will have several headnotes.[19] The text of the headnote may come from the text of the opinion or be written by the publisher. Because only the opinion itself is the primary authority, do not rely on the headnotes and do not cite them in legal documents.

Often a topic is attached to each headnote (if using a West reporter or WestlawNext, it is called a topic and key number; on Lexis Advance, it is called a topic). The topic can be used to find similar cases, as discussed in Chapter 5.

---

15. Other jurisdictions may call this party the respondent rather than the appellee.

16. In other jurisdictions, the court does not write this summary, so it is not authoritative. Sometimes the syllabus is called the synopsis of the case.

17. *See* Rep. O.R. 2.2.

18. Chapter 6 discusses how to find court documents.

19. *Ohio State Reports* does not have headnotes. *Ohio Appellate Reports* and *Ohio Miscellaneous Reports* have headnotes identical to those on WestlawNext and in the *North Eastern Reporter.*

Opinion. The opinion contains the actual decision and reasoning of the court. If the judges who heard the case do not agree on the outcome or the reasons for the outcome, one case may have several opinions. The opinion supported by a majority of the judges is called the *majority opinion.* An opinion written to agree with the outcome but not the reasoning of the majority is called a *concurring opinion.* Opinions written by judges who disagree with the outcome supported by the majority of the judges are called *dissenting opinions.* While only the majority opinion is binding precedent, the other opinions provide valuable insights and may be cited as persuasive authority. If there is no majority on both the outcome and the reasoning, the case will be decided by whichever opinion garners the most support and is called a *plurality decision.*

Disposition. At the end of each opinion, the disposition of the case appears, which states the court's decision to affirm, reverse, remand, or vacate the decision below. If the appellate court agrees with only part of the lower court's decision, it may affirm in part and reverse in part.

VII. Reading and Analyzing Cases

After locating a case, you must read it, understand it, and analyze its potential relevance to the problem you are researching. This process may take more mental work than you have ever dedicated to just a few pages of text. It is not unusual for a lawyer to spend hours reading and re-reading a complex case. For a novice, this reading is frequently interrupted by referring to a law dictionary to try to understand the terms used.

To aid your early efforts at reading cases, the following sections explain basic concepts of civil procedure and case analysis. The chapter ends with strategies for reading cases effectively.

A. Brief Overview of Civil Procedure

A person who believes that he has been harmed begins civil litigation by filing a *complaint* in a court he chooses. The *plaintiff* is the person who files the complaint; the person against whom the complaint is filed is the *defendant.* The complaint names the parties, states the facts, notes the relevant laws, and asks for relief. Courts vary considerably in how much information is required at this stage of the litigation. In general, the complaint must be specific enough to put the defendant on notice of the legal concerns at issue and to allow her to prepare a defense.

The defendant has a limited amount of time in which to file a response to this complaint. (If the defendant does nothing within the prescribed time, the plaintiff can ask the court for a *default judgment*, which would grant the plaintiff the relief sought in the complaint.) One form of response to the complaint is an answer. In the answer, the defendant admits to the parts of the complaint that she knows are true, denies those things that she disputes, and asserts no knowledge of the remaining allegations. The defendant also may raise affirmative defenses.

Throughout the litigation, parties submit a variety of papers to the court for its consideration. Some require no action or response from the court, for example, the filing of the complaint. In other instances, a party asks the court to make a decision or take action. An example is a *motion for summary judgment*, where a party asks the court to decide in that party's favor without the need for a trial.

When the trial judge grants a motion that ends a case, the losing party can appeal. The appealing party is called the *appellant*; the other party is the *respondent*. In deciding an appeal from an order granting a motion, the appellate court is deciding whether the trial judge was correct in issuing the order at that stage in the litigation. If the appellate court agrees with the decision of the trial judge, it will *affirm*. If not, the court will *reverse* the order granting the motion and in some instances *remand* the case back to the trial court.

Even at trial, the parties might make motions that can be appealed. For example, during the trial, the plaintiff presents his evidence first. After all of the plaintiff's witnesses have testified, the defendant may now move for a *judgment as a matter of law*, arguing that the plaintiff cannot win based on the evidence presented and asking for an immediate decision. An order granting that motion could be appealed.

Most reported cases are appeals of orders granting motions. Courts apply different *standards of review* to these cases, which depend on the motion that has been appealed. While standards of review are beyond the scope of this book, understanding the procedural posture of the case is crucial to understanding the court's holding. The relevant rules of civil procedure will guide your analysis. Texts listed in Appendix D contain helpful explanations as well.

B. Analyzing the Substance of the Case

Early in your career, it may be difficult to determine whether a case is relevant to your research problem. If the case concerns the same legally significant facts as your client's situation and the court applies law on point for your problem, then the case is legally relevant. *Legally significant facts* are those that affect the court's decision. Some attorneys call these *outcome-determinative facts* or *key facts*. Which facts are legally significant depends on the case. The height of the defendant in a contract dispute is unlikely to be legally significant, but that fact may be critical in a criminal case where the only eyewitness testified that the thief was about five feet tall.

Rarely will research reveal a case with facts that are exactly the same as your client's situation. Rather, several cases may involve facts that are similar to your client's situation but not exactly the same. Your job is to determine whether the facts are similar enough for a court to apply the law in the same way and reach the same outcome. If the court reached a decision favorable to your client, you will highlight the similarities. If, however, the court reached a decision unfavorable to your client, you may distinguish the case from yours by highlighting differences in the facts, or argue that the court's reasoning is faulty. You have an ethical duty to ensure that the court knows about a case directly on point, even if the outcome of that case is adverse to your client.

It is also unlikely that one case will address all aspects of your client's situation. Most legal claims have several elements or factors. *Elements* are required subparts of a claim, while *factors* are important aspects, but not required. If a court decides that one element is not met, it may not discuss others. In a different case, the court may decide that two factors are so overwhelming that others have no impact on the outcome. In these circumstances, you would have to find additional cases that analyze the other elements or factors.

Once you determine that a case is relevant to some portion of your analysis, you must decide how heavily it will weigh in your analysis. Two important points need to be considered here. One is the concept of *stare decisis*; the other is the difference between the holding of the case and dicta within that case.

Stare decisis means "to stand by things decided."[20] This means that courts must follow prior opinions of courts within a given jurisdiction. Thus, the Courts of Appeals in Ohio must follow the decisions of the Supreme Court of Ohio, but not opinions of courts in other states. The Ohio Courts of Appeals are divided into twelve districts.[21] The Court of Appeals in a particular district must follow opinions decided in that district, but need not follow those of another district.

---

20. *Black's Law Dictionary* 1537 (9th ed. 2014).

21. See www.supremecourt.ohio.gov/JudSystem/districtCourts/default.asp for a map detailing the jurisdiction of these courts.

Under *stare decisis*, courts are required to follow the holding of prior cases to ensure consistency in the application of the law. However, a court may decide to stop following its earlier cases because societal changes have outdated the law or because a new statute has been enacted that changed the legal landscape.

The *holding* is the court's ultimate decision on the matter of law at issue in the case. Other statements or observations included in the opinion are not binding; they are referred to as *dicta*. For example, a court in a property dispute may hold that the land belongs to Martinez. In reaching that decision, the court may note that, had the facts been slightly different, it would have decided the land belonged to Chernov. That observation is not binding on future courts, though it might be cited as persuasive authority.

After finding a number of cases that have similar facts, that discuss the same legal issue, and that are binding on your client's case, the next step is to synthesize the cases to state and explain the rule. Sometimes a court states the rule fully; if not, piece together the information from the relevant cases to state the rule completely but concisely. Then use the analysis and facts of various cases to explain the law. Decide how the rule and explanation of the law apply to your client's facts and determine your conclusion. Note that this method of synthesis is much more than mere summaries of all the various cases. Legal analysis texts in Appendix D of this book explain synthesis in detail.

C. Strategies for Reading Cases

As you begin reading cases, the following strategies may help you understand them more quickly and more thoroughly.

- Review the syllabus quickly to determine whether the case seems to be on point. If so, skim the headnotes to find the particular portion of the case that is relevant. Remember that one case may discuss several issues of law, only one or two of which may interest you. Go to the portion of the case identified by the relevant headnote and decide whether it is important for your project.

- If the case is on point, skim the entire case to get a feeling for what happened and why, focusing on the portion of the case identified by the relevant headnote.

- Read the case slowly and carefully. Skip the parts that are obviously not pertinent to your client's problem. For example, when researching a property question, there is no need to scrutinize the tort issue that is not pertinent to your property question.

- At the end of each paragraph or page, pause and consider what you have read. If you cannot summarize it, try reading the material again.

- The next time you read the case, take notes. The notes may be a formal "case brief" or they may be scribbles that only you can understand. Regardless of the form, the process of taking notes will help you parse through, identify, and comprehend the essential concepts of the case. In law school, the notes will record your understanding of the case both for class discussion and for the end of the semester when you begin to review for exams. When preparing to write a legal document, the notes will assist you in organizing your analysis into an outline.

- Note that skimming text online or highlighting a printed page is often not sufficient to achieve a thorough comprehension of judicial opinions.

Often you will read groups of cases as you conduct research. Reading the cases and understanding the law will be easier with an organized approach. First, organize groups of cases according to jurisdiction and then by decision date. Learning how the law developed over time in each jurisdiction will be easier if you read the cases chronologically. Finding the current rule of law will likely be easier if you begin with the most recent cases. Define your goal and organize the order in which you read the cases accordingly.

Pay attention to how the cases fit together. Look for trends in the law and in the facts of the cases. Has the law remained unchanged or have new elements been introduced? Has the meaning of an important term been redefined? Have certain facts virtually guaranteed success for one party while other facts have tended to cause difficulties? Does one case summarize the current rule or do you have to synthesize a rule from several cases that each address part of the rule?

Using some combination of the strategies described above will improve your comprehension of the cases that you read and their applicability to the problem that you are researching.

Chapter 5

Finding and Updating Cases

I. Researching Cases Generally

One of the most important, yet difficult, parts of legal research is finding cases on a particular topic. This chapter describes two methods for finding cases on a legal issue: full-text searching and topic-based searching.[1] Each method plays a distinct part in effective legal research. Full-text searching simply finds a combination of words and phrases in a particular set of cases. For example, a search for the phrase "death penalty" may only return cases that include that phrase; it may not include cases where the court used the phrase "capital punishment," even though both phrases describe the same idea. Topic-based searching finds cases on a particular topic or locates similar cases. When searching for capital punishment cases by topic, you will find capital punishment cases grouped together, regardless of the words used to describe this idea.

In addition to full-text and topic-based searching, other ways to find cases include finding citations to relevant cases in existing cases and through finding tools and citators. For example, you may begin research with a known, relevant case and use it to find more cases. You could use a finding tool like "Words and Phrases" to identify cases in which a court has defined a particular word or phrase you know is relevant. Another way to find cases is through updating with citators. While the primary purpose of updating is to determine whether a case is still respected legal authority, citators list all cases that have cited the case being updated. Thus, the process is likely to uncover additional cases that are relevant to a particular research project.

---

1. Other ways of researching cases are discussed in other chapters: annotated statutory codes list cases that interpret and apply statutes (Chapter 3) and secondary sources that cover the topic refer to cases either in text or in footnotes (Chapter 9).

This chapter discusses each method in turn: full-text searching, online topic searching, searches that begin with a known case or an undefined term, and updating. An appendix to this chapter explains using print digests to find cases.

II. Full-Text Searching

A. Types of Searches

The search functions used for full-text searching fall into two broad categories: natural-language searching and terms-and-connectors searching. Brief explanations of each search method appear below. Additionally, most online services provide guidance about how to build effective searches. For example, the Supreme Court of Ohio's website contains a one-page description of search help that describes the search logic and filters available on the site.[2] Likewise, Bloomberg Law, Lexis Advance, and WestlawNext offer extensive tutorials and other materials to explain how to search on those sites.

Natural-language searching is similar to Google searching. The researcher types in key words or a description of a legal issue, and the program applies an algorithm to select the best results.

In a terms-and-connectors search, the legal researcher develops key words and then uses connectors to describe how the words should appear together. A list of the frequently used connectors and commands from the major commercial services appears in Table 5-1; many of these same terms and connectors also work with the free services.

Most services, both commercial and free, allow for searching particular portions of documents (e.g., case name, judge, date) instead of searching entire documents. On Bloomberg Law and WestlawNext, these document parts are called *fields*, and on Lexis Advance, they are called *segments*.

Both Bloomberg Law and WestlawNext incorporate search templates that allow you to type a search into a box for the particular field or fields you wish to search. The service then will create a search that incorporates that field search with your search. For example, if you want to search for Ohio Supreme Court opinions about eminent domain that are written by former Chief Justice Moyer, you could type "eminent domain" into the main search box and Moyer

---

2. *See Opinion Search Site Help*, The Supreme Court of Ohio, http://www.sco net.state.oh.us/ROD/docs/Help.aspx#FullText.

Table 5-1. Connectors and Commands for Online Searching

Goal	Bloomberg Law	Lexis Advance	WestlawNext
To find alternative terms anywhere in the document	or	or	or blank space
To find both terms anywhere in the document	and	and &	and &
To find both terms within a particular distance from each other	/p = within one paragraph /s = within one sentence /n = within *n* words np/ = within specified range in specified order	/p = within one paragraph /s = within one sentence /n = within *n* words	/p = within one paragraph /s = within one sentence /n = within *n* words
To find terms used as a phrase	Put the phrase in quotation marks	Leave a blank space between each word	Put the phrase in quotation marks
To control the hierarchy of searching	parentheses	parentheses	parentheses
To exclude terms	not and not but not	and not	but %
To extend the end of a term	!	!	!
To hold the place of letters in a term	*	* ?	*

into the "written by" field. WestlawNext would turn your search into this: "eminent domain" and WB(Moyer) — you will see the abbreviation for the field and the parenthetical in the search box. On Bloomberg Law, you could create an identical search, but the field searching happens behind the scenes — the field search does not get appended to your primary search in the same way that it does in WestlawNext.

WestlawNext offers many fields, but the fields vary by content type. To see the full range of available search fields, you must first choose a content type. When at the home screen, the fields available via advance search are limited to those fields that are common to all content types. Fields in Bloomberg Law also vary by content type.

The Lexis Advance counterparts to fields are called document *segments*. Unlike fields on other services, Lexis Advance segments do not appear as a part of the initial or the advanced search screens. The researcher can, however, use segments as a part of her terms-and-connectors search. Available segments for case searching on Lexis Advance are *cite, name, court, summary, number, judges, written by*, and *attorney*. Thus, you could find the eminent domain opinions by Chief Justice Moyer on Lexis Advance with a search that looks like this: "eminent domain" and writtenby(Moyer).

B. Narrowing Results with Limits or Filters

To focus your results, you can use limits and filters. You can apply these limits both before and after your initial search. For example, to find the eminent domain cases written by Chief Justice Moyer, you could limit your search to just Ohio Supreme Court opinions from the outset. That is, before you search, you could limit or filter your search to just opinions of the Ohio Supreme Court. Not all services, provide this pre-search filter, but the Ohio Supreme Court's website, Bloomberg Law, and WestlawNext all do. On Lexis Advance, you would have to first run a broader search of Ohio cases and then narrow that search to focus on just opinions from the Supreme Court.

Once you have run your initial search, the commercial providers allow you to further narrow your search. In other words, you can select post-search limits or filters as well. In Lexis Advance, you would use those post-search filters to further narrow the results to Ohio Supreme Court opinions. All three major commercial services offer varied options to further narrow results, many of which are similar and can be accomplished by clicking a link or checking a box.

On Lexis Advance and WestlawNext, you can also narrow your search by running other searches within the search results. Both services call this "Search within results," and you can find a "Search within results" search box in the options for narrowing search results.

C. Choosing What to Read

When an effective search retrieves a large number of cases, or when faced with tight deadlines, you may have to be selective in choosing the cases to read. First, read those cases that are binding authority in your jurisdiction. Within that subset, read the most recent cases. If you have to winnow further, prioritize cases with similar facts.

III. Online Subject Searching

In addition to full-text searching, both WestlawNext and Lexis Advance offer alternative approaches to finding cases. WestlawNext's digest system, a well-developed subject index to case law, provides one approach to finding cases. Lexis Advance also allows for searching through its legal topics and headnotes. Bloomberg Law includes its own headnotes on some cases, and those headnotes are organized into "Classification Outlines." As of this writing, however, the Bloomberg Law headnotes and topical classification system are not fully developed.

A. Topical Searching on WestlawNext

1. West's Key Number Digest

The "West Key Number System" on WestlawNext contains West's vast case law digest system. It facilitates subject searching by organizing American law into broad *topics* and then narrower subtopics, called *key numbers*. Examples of topics include "Adoption," "Civil Rights," "Constitutional Law," and "Treason." An example of a topic and key number relating to the First Amendment right to free speech in airports is "Constitutional Law 1767." The key number 1767 refers to the subtopic "Freedom of Speech, Expression, and Press — Airports, aviation and airspace."

"Constitutional Law" is a vast topic containing over 4000 key numbers on subtopics such as amendment of the constitution, construction of constitutional provisions, and constitutional rights (including the bill of rights and the equal protection amendment). An example of a much shorter topic is "Treason," which includes just 14 key numbers on subtopics such as the elements of treason, defenses, and trial procedure in treason cases.

To search for a relevant topic and key number, use the "Key Numbers" feature on WestlawNext. After finding a relevant topic and key number, such as "Adoption 25" on foreign adoption, select a particular jurisdiction to search. You may also add key words to the search. Results may be ordered to see the most recent cases or the most cited cases first. The "most recent" choice will retrieve the latest cases that use the headnotes. The "most cited" feature will find the headnotes that have been cited by the most cases. The advantage to using the "most cited" feature is finding important or seminal cases on a particular topic, which will be listed first.

When using online digests, search results will often be in headnote form. As a case is published, attorney editors working for a publisher identify each point of law in the case and write a headnote that summarizes the point of law. In WestlawNext, each headnote is assigned a topic and key number. Although the language may be copied directly from the text of the case, headnotes are not authoritative and should never be cited.

The topic and key number or headnote can also be added to a full-text search. This is helpful when the topic is too broad to be used alone or when adding key words would narrow the results to cases with particular facts.

2. Practice Areas

WestlawNext also allows searching by topic in a number of practice areas such as "Bankruptcy," "Insurance," and "Taxation." While the service is broader than case searching (including statutes, administrative material, and secondary sources), the topic search allows you to zero in on cases that are restricted to your subject.

From the WestlawNext home page, click on the "Practice Areas" tab to see the list of topics. These topics may be broken down into subtopics. For example, to search Ohio family law cases, select the "Family Law" topic, then choose "Family Law Cases" from the listed content types and select "Ohio" as the jurisdiction in the jurisdiction selector just to the right of the search box. Any search you now run will deliver results restricted to Ohio cases concerning family law.

B. Topical Searching on Lexis Advance

Lexis Advance offers research by legal topic using the "Browse" feature, which appears in the Lexis Advance header. Browse allows you to search for a topic by typing in key terms or by browsing a topic hierarchy that functions much like West's topic and key number system. For example, typing in the word "adoption" will result two broad topics: "family law" and "labor & employment." Selecting "family law" will produce a list of different subtopics such as "grandparent," "stepparent," and "private adoptions."

In addition to allowing searching, "Browse" includes an extensive outline of the law, beginning with broad categories like "Bankruptcy Law" and "Contracts Law." Clicking on a broad category will expand it to show more focused headings within that category. Once you select a more focused subtopic within a broader area of law, Lexis will present possible actions, which include (1) get a document, (2) add topic as search filter, and (3) create a topic alert.

Headnotes offer another way to search by topic on Lexis Advance. If you find a useful Lexis headnote, you can select a topic link in the headnote and Lexis Advance will present the same options available when exploring topics in "Browse": (1) get documents, (2) add the topic as a search filter, and (3) create a topic alert. Notably, Lexis headnotes are not identical to Westlaw headnotes or to headnotes in West reporters. West's editorial staff writes the West headnotes; Lexis Advance headnotes use language taken directly from the cases themselves. Just like West headnotes, though, Lexis headnotes should be relied up on as a research tool, only. You must read the opinion itself to understand the content of the headnote in context.

Lexis Advance also has topical collections of sources that include cases. You can select topical collections by selecting the "Practice Area and Topic" filter at the Lexis Advance home screen.

IV. Starting with a Relevant Case

If you begin research knowing one case on point, you can take advantage of other features of WestlawNext and Lexis Advance to find additional cases on point.

Because the West headnote system is uniform across jurisdictions, a case from any jurisdiction can quickly lead to a relevant case in the proper jurisdiction. Use the hyperlinked topics and key numbers in the case's headnotes. After clicking on a hyperlinked topic or key number, choose the jurisdiction you wish to search and then choose to list the results by "most recent" or "most cited."

On Lexis Advance, you can also use a single relevant case to find other relevant cases. Clicking on a hyperlinked topic in a Lexis headnote will bring up search options, including "get documents," which will deliver diverse materials that cover the topic. Once you select "get documents," you can then filter and search within results to find cases relevant to your research.

V. Using Words and Phrases

While a dictionary like *Black's Law Dictionary* will provide a general definition of a term, Words and Phrases will lead to cases that define the term for a particular jurisdiction. Judicial definitions are especially helpful when an important term in a statute is vague.

This tool exists both online and in print. To learn whether a court has defined a term, use the Word & Phrases (WP) field when searching cases in a WestlawNext. This feature does not exist on Lexis Advance. Alternatively, many academic law libraries have the comprehensive *Words and Phrases* set in print (published by Thomson Reuters) and most print digests have a Words & Phrases volume.

VI. Updating Cases with Citators

Because courts issue new opinions every day and the legislature can change a law at any time, updating case law research is essential.[3] Updating a case requires finding every subsequent case that has cited the case and any statute that supersedes the case. A *citator* provides a list of these cases and statutes. The citator service on Bloomberg Law is called "BCite," on WestlawNext it is called "KeyCite," and on Lexis Advance it is called "Shepard's."[4] When updating a case, the case that is being updated is called the *cited reference* or *cited case* while the cases that were decided later and refer to the cited case are called the *citing references* or *citing cases*.

Each citator delivers two categories of information about the cited case: (1) *history* and (2) *treatment*. History (also called direct history and appellate history) tells what happened to the cited case both before and after the cited case was decided. In other words, history involves what happened to particular case up and down the chain on appeal. Everything else reported by the citators fits into the *treatment* category. Treatment includes any time the cited case is mentioned in another source.

Regardless of the citator service being used, the process of updating a case is similar. This process is summarized in Table 5-2.

Table 5-2. Outline for Updating Cases

1. Pull up the case to be updated in Bloomberg Law, Lexis, or Westlaw.

2. Analyze the citator symbol describing the case (e.g., red flag or stop sign) to learn about the history and treatment of the cited case.

3. Review the treatment of the cited case by the citing references and choose which cases to read based upon the citing reference's treatment, jurisdiction, date, or legal topic.

4. Read the appropriate cases and evaluate (a) how they affect the authority of the cited case and (b) whether they are useful for analyzing your research project.

---

3. Other authorities can be updated, but the citators discussed in this chapter are most often used to update cases.

4. Shepard's was the first citator service, so the updating process is often referred to as "Shepardizing." Print citators still exist, but they are becoming obsolete in practice. If you are ever faced with having to use a print citator, such as *Shepard's Ohio Citations* or *Shepard's Ohio Unreported Appellate Citations*, refer to its table of contents and preface, which include detailed instructions.

First, using any of the three services described here, find the case you need to update. Remember that the case that you are updating is called the cited case. Bloomberg Law and WestlawNext display the history and treatment of a case using tabs across the top of the screen displaying the cited case. To get the same information on Lexis Advance, you need only select "Shepardize this document" on the right side of the search results window. Lexis Advance will take you to a separate screen that displays the history of the cited case and includes links to the treatment of the cited case by other authorities.

Your second step in using citators, right after finding the case, should be to analyze the symbol provided by the citator. Each of these online citators includes a symbol that tells you how the service's editors have categorized the status of the case. In general, red and yellow symbols suggest negative treatment (e.g., the cited case has been reversed, overruled, or criticized). Blue and green symbols suggest positive treatment (e.g., the cited case has been followed). Never rely upon the symbol alone. It is the responsibility of the researcher (not Bloomberg Law, or Lexis Advance, or WestlawNext) to determine whether a case still represents current law. This determination can be complicated and can take some time. The symbols are only a starting point. Table 5-3 explains the major signals that appear on BCite, Shepard's, and KeyCite.

Third, determine which citing references to read. Based on the number of citing references, determine whether you will review the full list or limit it. A citing reference list can be quite lengthy. For example, the landmark case of *Roe v. Wade* has over 23,000 citing references on KeyCite, over 17,000 citing references on Shepard's, and well over 3,000 cases on BCite (plus many more other sources). It would be neither an effective nor an efficient research strategy to read all of these sources.

All three services allow you to narrow the citing references by things like content type, date, court, and jurisdiction. The services also allow you to search within results, so you can perform a focused search of the citing references to obtain the most relevant cases to read. Factors to consider when choosing which sources to read include (1) the type and depth treatment of the cited case by each source, (2) the jurisdiction, (3) the type of document, (4) the date, and (5) the headnotes cited. Each of these factors is explained below.

Treatment. One of the most important factors in determining whether the case is still good law is the treatment of the cited case by the citing references. Cases that treat the cited reference negatively are most important. A review of recent negative cases will show whether courts still rely on the legal principles of the cited case. Although treated as negative references, cases that distinguish the cited reference are very helpful regardless of their outcome. They can help

Table 5-3. Selected Signals of Online Citators

BCite Symbol Bloomberg Law	KeyCite Symbol WestlawNext	Shepard's Symbol Lexis Advance	Meaning
Red minus sign	Red flag	Red stop sign	Strong negative treatment, e.g., a point of law has been overruled.
No equivalent	No equivalent	Orange Q	The source's continuing validity has been questioned.
Yellow triangle	Yellow flag	Yellow triangle	Possible negative treatment.
Green plus sign (The green plus sign is also used when there are no citing cases.)	No equivalent	Green plus sign	Positive treatment.
No equivalent	No equivalent	Blue A	Citing references with analysis.
No equivalent	Blue striped flag	No equivalent	Cited case has been appealed to U.S. Courts of Appeals or U.S. Supreme Court.
Blue slash	No equivalent	No equivalent	One or more cases distinguish cited case on law or facts.

explain the legal rule at issue, provide examples of how courts have applied a rule, and show in what factual situations the courts have determined that the rule does not apply. Table 5-4 explains the more important treatments.

A related factor is the depth of treatment. Each service — BCite, Shepard's, and KeyCite — indicates how much attention the citing reference gives to the cited case through their depth-of-treatment bars. Generally, the longer the bar (green in KeyCite and blue in BCite and Shepard's), the more likely a citing case discusses the cited case in depth.

Table 5-4. Selected Types of Treatment in Online Citators

Treatment	Explanation
Overruled	The citing reference expressly disapproves of the cited case and has the authority to hold that the case no longer has the force of law.
Criticized	The citing reference disapproves of the cited case, but may not have the authority to overrule the case.
Distinguished	The citing reference differs from the cited case, especially regarding the legally significant facts.
Followed	The citing reference expressly relies on the cited case.

Jurisdiction. The jurisdiction of the citing references is virtually as important as the treatment. Cases in your jurisdiction may be mandatory authority, and you must find any mandatory authority that overrules, reverses, or otherwise treats negatively the cited case.

Type of Document. BCite, Shepard's, and KeyCite include many types of citing references, such as cases, statutes, court briefs, and secondary sources. Each of these documents will be important to you throughout your research. Cases and statutes help determine whether the cited case is still good law. Court briefs and law review articles provide possible arguments and novel legal theories. When pressed for time, start with cases and statutes to determine whether your cited case is still respected.

Date. If a case has been cited numerous times, you may decide to read cases from just the past 10 years. Or, if you have updated the case previously in a project that you have worked on for several months, you may restrict the results to just those since the previous time you updated.

Headnote. Most cases include discussions of many legal topics. For example, a divorce case may include whether grounds for divorce exist, a division of marital property, and a determination of the custody of children and spousal support; the case might also address procedural issues like summary judgment. If you are examining the cited reference for a particular legal issue, you will want to narrow the citing references to only those that discuss that issue, which you can identify by filtering or narrowing by headnotes.

The final step in updating cases is to read the appropriate citing references and determine whether the case should be relied on. This step can be difficult and time consuming, but ethical rules require that attorneys rely only on the current law.

VII. Citing Cases

Table 5-5 provides examples for citing an Ohio case pursuant to the *ALWD Guide*, the *Bluebook*, and the *Ohio Manual of Citations*. Notice that all three citations include the WebCite, which is Ohio's public domain citation for cases published on the Supreme Court of Ohio's website.

Table 5-5. Ohio Case Citation Examples

Citation Method	Example	Source
ALWD Guide	*Welling v. Weinfeld*, 113 Ohio St. 3d 464, 2007-Ohio-2451, 866 N.E.2d 1051.	Rule 12 and Appendix 1(B)
Bluebook	*Welling v. Weinfeld*, 113 Ohio St. 3d 464, 2007-Ohio-2451, 866 N.E.2d 1051.	Rule 10 and Table T1
Ohio Manual of Citations	*Welling v. Weinfeld*, 113 Ohio St.3d 464, 2007-Ohio-2451, 866 N.E.2d 1051.	Page 14

Appendix: West Print Digests

This appendix covers West digests because they are the most widely used print digests. Much of the information provided here applies to other case digests as well.[5]

The West print digest system uses the same topics and key numbers as the WestlawNext version discussed earlier in this chapter. The digest entries under

---

5. In 2010, LexisNexis ceased publishing its digest to Ohio case law, called *Anderson's Ohio Case Locator*. An index to cases published in *Ohio State Reports*, *Ohio Appellate Reports*, and *Ohio Miscellaneous Reports*, it was much less detailed than *West's Ohio Digest* (it was a single-volume work, while *West's Ohio Digest* has over 80 volumes) and covered cases only back to 1991. It is still a useful tool to find relevant cases from that period.

each topic and key number are the actual headnotes found in cases. Each headnote is assigned a topic and key number. Figure 5-A provides an excerpt of

Figure 5-A. Excerpt from a Case in West's *North Eastern Reporter*

1090 Ohio 696 NORTH EASTERN REPORTER, 2d SERIES

120 Ohio App.3d 88

⌐₈₈In re HITCHCOCK et al.*

Nos. 69291, 69292.

Court of Appeals of Ohio,
Eighth District, Cuyahoga County.

Decided Nov. 21, 1996.

Cuyahoga County Department of Children and Family Services (CCDCFS) placed children adjudicated neglected with elder sibling's adoptive parents, rather than with white foster parents who had initially been given custody of one child and who wished to adopt both children. Foster parents intervened. Adoptive parents filed motions for legal custody of both children. The Common Pleas Court of Cuyahoga County, Juvenile Court Division, terminated CCDCFS's permanent custody and granted legal custody to adoptive parents. Foster parents appealed. On consolidation of actions, the Court of Appeals, Spellacy, C.J., held that: (1) juvenile court did not abuse its discretion by permitting adoptive parents to remain as parties to custody proceeding despite their ineligibility to adopt; (2) foster parents had sufficient notice of issues to be addressed and sufficient opportunity to present evidence and witnesses; (3) foster parents had standing to appeal from juvenile court's order; and (4) juvenile court's order was in effect denial of foster parents' adoption petition and as such exceeded that court's jurisdiction.

Reversed and remanded.

1. Infants ⟨key⟩19.3(1)

Juvenile court has wide discretion in affording any individual party status in proceeding for custody. Juvenile Procedure Rule 2.

2. Infants ⟨key⟩19.3(7)

Abuse of juvenile court's discretion in granting party status to individual in custody proceeding connotes more than error of law or judgment; it implies court's attitude was

unreasonable, arbitrary, or unconscionable. Juvenile Procedure Rule 2.

⌐₈₉3. Infants ⟨key⟩230.1

Juvenile court did not abuse its discretion by permitting couple legally ineligible to adopt children to remain as parties to post-dispositional custody proceeding while court examined merits of couple's motion for legal custody; motion presented additional disposition option, which court was required to consider as part of its obligation to consider best interests of children.

4. Appeal and Error ⟨key⟩907(1)

If trial court fails to rule upon motion, it will be presumed that motion was overruled.

5. Infants ⟨key⟩230.1

Foster parents had sufficient notice of issues to be addressed in post-dispositional custody proceeding, and sufficient opportunity to present evidence and witnesses, to permit them effectively to oppose adoptive parents' motion for legal custody; trial court repeatedly stated that proceeding was one for custody review, and foster parents' opposition to motion for legal custody indicated their awareness of issue concerning whether legal custody should be given to adoptive parents.

6. Appeal and Error ⟨key⟩169

Appellate court will not consider any error which complaining party could have called to court's attention at time alleged error could have been avoided or corrected by trial court.

7. Infants ⟨key⟩230.1

No new finding of dependency is required based upon circumstances of current placement of child before trial court may consider motion to modify or change dispositional order, as juvenile court retains jurisdiction following initial dispositional hearing until child reaches age of majority or is adopted, and may therefore hold additional hearings sua sponte or on motion of any party to reconsider original order. R.C. §§ 2151.353(E)(1, 2), 2151.417(A, B).

* Reporter's Note: A discretionary appeal to the Supreme Court of Ohio was dismissed as having

been improvidently allowed in (1998), 81 Ohio St.3d 1222, 689 N.E.2d 43.

the case *In re Hitchcock*, which includes the headnotes summarizing the key legal concepts of the case.

The scope of most West digests is based upon jurisdiction, though there are some topic-based digests, such as the *Education Law Digest*. The current digest used for researching Ohio law is *West's Ohio Digest*. It includes headnotes of cases from state courts in Ohio, the Sixth Circuit, and the United States Supreme Court that originated in Ohio. The digest also includes references to secondary sources, such as legal encyclopedias and law review articles. An example of entries in *West's Ohio Digest* is given in Figure 5-B.

Figure 5-B. Excerpts from *West's Ohio Digest* "Adoption"

Ohio 1964. Generally, one person will be considered as adopted child of another if there is established or created between them status or legal relationship of parent and child, but that status or relationship can be established or created only by statutory provisions.

In re Gompf's Estate, 195 N.E.2d 806, 175 Ohio St. 400, 25 O.O.2d 388.

Ohio App. 4 Dist. 1991. "Adoption" creates relationship of parent and child while severing parental rights and responsibilities of biological or other legal parents; adoption is not proceeding to determine custody.

In re Adoption of Howell, 601 N.E.2d 92, 77 Ohio App.3d 80.

Ohio App. 8 Dist. 1996. Goal of adoption statutes is to protect best interests of the children; cornerstone of adoption statutes is promotion of children's welfare, specifically those children who lack and who are in need of security and benefits of loving home and family.

In re Hitchcock, 696 N.E.2d 1090, 120 Ohio App.3d 88.

Source: *West's Ohio Digest*. Reprinted with permission of West, a Thomson Reuters business.

West publishes regional digests for some of its regional reporters. Ohio cases were contained in the *North Eastern Digest*, but that publication ceased with the 1971 update. The most focused print digest for Ohio research is *West's Ohio Digest*. Table 5-A lists several digests that may be useful to Ohio legal researchers.

West's Ohio Digest includes cases since 1803, the year Ohio became a state. In other words, it is a cumulative digest. Many other digests contain cases from only a certain period of time. To do thorough research in non-cumulative digests such as the *Federal Practice Digest*, you may have to consult more than one series.

Table 5-A. Selected Digests

Title	Coverage
West's Ohio Digest	Cases from Ohio courts and federal courts in Ohio (and appellate review of those cases)
Decennial Digest	Cases from all jurisdictions included in West's national reporter system
Federal Practice Digest	Cases from United States District Courts, United States Courts of Appeal, and the United States Supreme Court (and some topical federal reporters)
United States Supreme Court Digest	Cases from the United States Supreme Court

In a state digest, headnotes are arranged under each topic and key number according to the court that decided each case. Federal cases are listed first, followed by state court cases. Within the federal and state systems, cases are listed according to judicial hierarchy: cases from the highest appellate court are listed first, followed by decisions of intermediate appellate courts, then trial court cases. Cases from each court are given in reverse chronological order. At the end of each digest headnote are citations to any statutes that are cited in the case. This information is followed by the case citation, including subsequent history, and any parallel citations.

There are several approaches for using print digests to conduct legal research. The best approach depends on the information available when beginning your research and what you need to find.

1. Searching for a Legal Issue with the Descriptive-Word Index

Most often you will begin your research with a fact pattern and a legal issue, but without any cases on point and without knowing which topics and key numbers may be relevant. In these situations, use the Descriptive-Word Index to translate research terms into the topics and key numbers used by the digest to index cases relevant to your client's problem.

First, search for your research terms in the Descriptive-Word Index, a multi-volume index often shelved at the end of the digest. Write down the topic and key number for each term you find. Also check each volume's annual pocket parts for additional topics and key numbers. Figure 5-C shows an excerpt from the Descriptive-Word Index in *West's Ohio Digest*. Some topics are abbreviated in the Descriptive-Word Index. A list of topics and their abbreviations can be found at the front of each index volume. Be sure to record both the topic and key number. Many topics will have the same key numbers, so a number alone is not helpful.

Figure 5-C. Excerpts from the Descriptive-Word Index in *West's Ohio Digest*

ADOPTION   1 Ohio D-75

References are to Digest Topics and Key Numbers

ADOPTION OF PERSONS
ABANDONMENT
     Evidence, **Adop** 🔑 7.8(5)
     Forfeiting parent's rights, **Adop** 🔑 7.4(2.1, 3)
ACTIONS and proceedings, **Adop** 🔑 9.1-15
ADMISSIBILITY of evidence, consent, **Adop** 🔑 7.8(2)
ADULTS, adoption of **Adop** 🔑 5
AGENCIES,
     Liability,
          Breach of Contract, **Infants** 🔑 17
AGREEMENTS to adopt, **Adop** 🔑 6
APPEAL and error, **Adop** 🔑 6
APPROVAL by court, **Adop** 🔑 13
ATTORNEY and client,
     Right to counsel,
          Adoption proceedings, **Adop** 🔑 13
          Consenting to adoption, **Adop** 🔑 7.5
BEST interest of the child
     Examination and approval of court, **Adop** 🔑 13
BURDEN of proof, consent, **Adop** 🔑 7.8(1)

Source: *West's Ohio Digest*. Reprinted with permission of West, a Thomson Reuters business.

Take your list of topics and key numbers to the main digest volumes and find the volume that contains one of your topics. At the beginning of each topic is a list of "Subjects Included" as well as "Subjects Excluded and Covered by Other Topics." These lists will help you decide whether that topic is likely to index cases most relevant to your research. The list of excluded subjects may contain references to other topics found elsewhere in the digest.

After these lists is the key number outline of the topic, under the heading "Analysis," as seen in Figure 5-D. Longer topics will contain a short, summary outline and then a detailed outline. Take a moment to skim the Analysis outline to ensure that you found in the Descriptive-Word Index all the relevant key numbers within that topic.

Figure 5-D. Excerpts from *West's Ohio Digest* Analysis for Adoption

Analysis

1. Nature of the proceeding.
2. Constitutionality of statutes.
3. Statutory provisions.
4. Persons who may adopt others.
5. Persons who may be adopted.
6. Agreements to adopt.
7. Consent of parties.
8. Deed or declaration.
9. Judicial proceedings.
    9.1. In general.
10. Jurisdiction.
11. Petition and parties.
12. Notice.
13. Examination and approval
    by court.
14. Order or decree.
15. Review.
16. Setting aside or revoking adoption.
17. Evidence of adoption.
18. Status of adopted persons in
    general.
20. Rights, duties, and liabilities
    created in general.
21. Inheritance by adopted children.
22. Inheritance from adopted children.
23. Inheritance through adopted
    children.
24. Effect of adoption on property rights
    of surviving husband or wife.
25. Foreign adoption.

Source: *West's Ohio Digest.* Reprinted with permission of West, a Thomson Reuters business.

Then turn to each of the relevant key numbers and review the case headnotes there. Write down the citation for each case that you decide you need to read.

More recent digest information is often provided through pocket parts. If the updated information is too thick to fit into the pocket part, the publisher will instead provide a soft-cover volume of updated material, which will be shelved next to the volume it updates. These supplements are in turn updated using *cumulative supplementary pamphlets*. These pamphlets contain updates for all topics, so they generally are shelved after all of the volumes of the digest. The cover of a cumulative supplement will indicate both its publication date and the date of the pocket part it updates.

Finally, you may find coverage after these cumulative supplements by going to a particular reporter's most recent volumes and *advance sheets*, and using the digest contained in each.[6] Of course, there will always be some window of

---

6. A table at the beginning of each digest volume will indicate which reporter volumes are indexed there. Updating requires you to check the digest sections of subsequent volumes of the reporters.

time between publication and release of the most current information. For same day currency, you must go to an online database, such as Lexis Advance or WestlawNext.[7]

2. Starting with a Relevant Case

If you begin research knowing one case on point, you can take a shortcut that skips the Descriptive-Word Index. Read the case in a West reporter and identify the headnotes that are relevant to your issue. Note the topics and key numbers given for the relevant headnotes. Then select a digest volume containing one of the topics. Within that topic, find the key number given in the related headnote and review the cases indexed there. To ensure that you have found all relevant topic and key numbers, skim the Analysis outline of that topic.

3. Words & Phrases

To learn whether a court has defined a term, refer to the Words & Phrases volumes at the end of the digest.[8] See Figure 5-E for an example.

Figure 5-E. Excerpt from Words & Phrases in *West's Ohio Digest*

ADOPTION
Ohio App. 4 Dist. 1991. "Adoption" creates relationship of parent and child while severing parental rights and responsibilities of biological or other legal parents; adoption is not proceeding to determine custody. — In re Adoption of Howell, 601 N.E.2d 91, 77 Ohio App.3d 80, jurisdictional motion overruled 583 N.E.2d 1320, 62 Ohio St.3d 1508. — Adop 1, 20

Source: *West's Ohio Digest*. Reprinted with permission of West, a Thomson Reuters business.

At the end of each entry in the Words & Phrases volumes, West lists the topics and key numbers used for that case's headnotes. The example in Figure 5-E includes two: "Adoption 1" and "Adoption 20."

---

7. Although Lexis Advance has a similar headnote system, only WestlawNext allows you to continue research using West topics and key numbers.

8. West also produces a multi-volume set, *Words and Phrases*, containing court definitions from federal and state jurisdictions combined.

4. Table of Cases

A digest's Table of Cases lists all the cases indexed in that digest series by both the primary plaintiff's name and the primary defendant's name. This table is helpful when you do not know the citation to a relevant case but do know the name of one or both parties. The Table of Cases provides the full name of the case, the citation for the case, and the relevant topics and key numbers. After consulting the Table of Cases, either read the case in a reporter or continue working in the digest using the topics and key numbers to find more related cases.

Chapter 6

Researching Court Rules and Documents

I. Court Rules and Court Documents Generally

Every detail of litigation is governed by *court rules*, from the style of papers filed with the court to the way a trial and an appeal are conducted. For example, Rule 4 of the Ohio Rules of Appellate Procedure gives the losing party 30 days to file an appeal, provides details on what must be in the notice of appeal, and describes how that notice must be served on the opposing party and filed with the court. In addition to court rules, the Supreme Court of Ohio issues the Ohio Rules of Professional Conduct that detail the ethical responsibilities and regulate the conduct of all attorneys admitted to practice in Ohio.[1]

This chapter begins with a discussion of court and ethical rules, then covers how to locate court documents, such as orders and judgments.

II. Ohio and Federal Court Rules

Many different types of court rules govern Ohio and federal courts. Table 6-1 lists examples of these rules. There are often parallel Ohio and federal court rules covering the same topic, such as the Ohio Rules of Civil Procedure and the Federal Rules of Civil Procedure. To decide which rules apply, determine in which court the legal matter will be litigated. Ohio rules apply in Ohio state courts; federal rules apply in federal courts.

---

1. The Ohio Rules of Professional Conduct became effective on February 1, 2007. Conduct that occurred before the effective date is governed by the previous version of the rules, the Code of Professional Responsibility.

Table 6-1. Selected Court Rules Applicable to Ohio Courts

Rules of Civil Procedure (Federal and Ohio)

Rules of Criminal Procedure (Federal and Ohio)

Rules of Evidence (Federal and Ohio)

Rules of Appellate Procedure (Federal and Ohio)

Ohio Rules of Juvenile Procedure

Local Rules of Courts of Appeals (Ohio)

Rules of Practice of the Common Pleas Courts (Ohio)

Rules of the Court of Claims (Ohio)

Ohio Supreme Court Rules of Practice

Ohio Rules for the Government of the Bar

Ohio Rules of Professional Conduct

In addition, each court may have *local rules* that expand on the state or federal court rules or set more specific requirements. For example, the Franklin County Court of Common Pleas has promulgated rules that apply only to cases filed in that court. These rules require, for example, that the attorney registration number, address, and telephone number appear on all documents filed with the court. You must review the local rules before writing a document that will be filed in court or making a court appearance.

III. Researching Court Rules

Federal, state, and local rules may be found in numerous sources. Compilations of court rules, such as *West's Ohio Rules of Court* (available on WestlawNext) or *Anderson's Annotated Rules Governing the Courts of Ohio* (available on Lexis Advance), often contain all the federal and state court rules for a given jurisdiction, along with the available local court rules. Additionally, annotated statutory codes may contain federal or state court rules (e.g., *Baldwin's Ohio Revised Code Annotated* contains the Ohio court rules; the *United States Code Annotated* contains federal court rules).

Court rules have become increasingly available online through the respective court's website. Additionally, the Consortium of Ohio County Law Libraries maintains a database of Ohio rules.[2] Smaller jurisdictions, however, might not publish their local rules either online or in print. In that situation, the rules must be obtained from the clerk of court for that jurisdiction.

When researching federal and state court rules, it is best to start with the annotated version of the rules since the annotations will help you both understand the rule and the potential legal issues surrounding it. The process for finding and understanding a relevant court rule is summarized in Table 6-2.

Table 6-2. Overview of Court Rules Research Process

1. Develop a list of research terms.

2. Find and read the controlling rule by using an index or searching the full text of the rules.

3. Find cases that interpret or apply the rule using the annotations or other case-finding tools.

4. Update the rule to ensure that it hasn't been amended or ruled unconstitutional.

A. Develop a List of Research Terms

To begin researching court rules, develop a list of research terms. These are the words that are likely to be in the text of the rule itself or terms that the publisher has used to index the rule. Use the journalistic or TARPP approach, as explained in Chapter 1, or design a brainstorming approach that works for you.

B. Find and Read the Rule

If you have already found a citation to the relevant rule, go directly to the text of the rule. Court rules may be found within the annotated code or within a separate publication or database. To determine where a particular set of court rules appears, scan the table of contents for the entire code. For each publisher, the code is arranged the same in print and online.[3]

---

2. The address is http://cocll.ohio.gov/Links.

3. In *Baldwin's Ohio Revised Code Annotated*, the rules appear at the end of the code in volumes called "Rules of Court." LexisNexis is phasing out the inclusion of court rules in *Page's Ohio Revised Code Annotated*. Currently, some rules appear in titles of the code related to the rules. In the *United States Code Annotated*, the rules are located in the related titles. In the *United States Code Service*, the rules appear at the end of the code in separate "Court Rules" volumes.

Otherwise, there are three ways to find relevant court rules: (1) use the index to the statutory code or court rules publication, (2) browse the table of contents for the rules, or (3) do a full-text search online.

First, both the print versions and the WestlawNext version of *Baldwin's Ohio Revised Code Annotated* and *United States Code Annotated* have indexes.[4] Indexes are organized in alphabetical order by broad topic, with more narrow topics listed underneath each broad topic. Each print code has a multi-volume general index, which is updated every year, and shorter indexes at the end of each title. Remember to be both patient and flexible when using an index. If your research terms do not appear, consider synonyms or antonyms. Cross-references in an index direct the researcher to the proper terminology or a broader topic. For example, in an index the entry for "Judges–Appellate" redirects the researcher to "Court of Appeals."

Next, because the rules are often organized in a meaningful manner, browsing the table of contents for a set of rules is an effective way to find relevant rules. For example, the Rules of Civil Procedure are generally arranged by the stages of litigation, beginning with information about drafting, filing, and serving the complaint, and then covering trial and judgment. It is important to review neighboring rules for definitional sections, exceptions, and other related rules. To do so, review either the general table of contents found at the beginning of the rules or the more specific table of contents at the beginning of each section or title of the rules.

Finally, full-text searching in an online database is another way to locate relevant rules. When searching in an online database, combine relevant research terms to build a comprehensive search of the rules. (Review Chapter 5, Part II, on full-text searching.)

C. Find Cases that Interpret or Apply the Rule

Before using the rule in your legal analysis, find cases in which the rule was at issue so you can predict how the rule may be applied.

One simple way to find applicable cases is to use the case annotations to the rule. Do not rely on the case summaries in the annotations alone because they do not provide the full context of the case and occasionally contain in-

---

4. Currently, the LexisNexis online versions of *Page's Ohio Revised Code Annotated* and *United States Code Service* do not have an index.

complete or inaccurate information. Instead, use the citation at the end of the summary to locate and review the full case.

D. Update the Rule

Be sure you are using the current rule, as rules may change. The Ohio Supreme Court is charged with writing rules "governing the practice and procedure in all courts in the state."[5] The court must file these rules with the General Assembly, and if the General Assembly refrains from adopting a concurrent resolution of disapproval by a certain date, the rules become effective. The court posts all current rules and any proposed changes to the rules on its website.[6]

In the federal system, the Judicial Conference and the United States Supreme Court must approve changes before they become effective. Additionally, the United States Congress has an opportunity to enact or reject proposed new rules or amendments to existing rules. If it does not, the new rules or amendments take effect. The Administrative Office of the U.S. Courts publishes proposed changes to the federal rules as well as a guide to researching rule amendments.[7]

When using a print statutory code, look for amendments to existing rules or new rules in the pocket part and supplements. Unfortunately, neither Shepard's on Lexis Advance nor KeyCite on WestlawNext advises users of proposed amendments to rules.

IV. Citing Court Rules

A proper citation to a court rule contains the correct abbreviation of the rule and the rule number. Table 6-3 provides a full citation to Ohio Rule of Civil Procedure 59, which deals with motions for a new trial.

---

5. Ohio Const. art. IV, § 5(B).

6. Currently, this information is available at www.supremecourt.ohio.gov/ RuleAmendments.

7. The address is www.uscourts.gov. Click on "Rules & Policies" in the menu, and then either "Pending Rules Amendments" or "Proposed Amendments Published for Public Comment."

Table 6-3. Examples of Court Rule Citation

Citation Method	Example	Source
ALWD Guide	Ohio R. Civ. P. 59	Rule 16.1
Bluebook	Ohio R. Civ. P. 59	Rule 12.9.3 and Bluepages B12.1.3
Ohio Manual of Citations	Civ.R. 59	Rule 4.1

V. Rules of Professional Conduct

The Ohio Rules of Professional Conduct govern attorney practice, including all research done in legal matters. Rule 1.1 mandates that attorneys provide "competent representation to the client." This includes legal research and writing. Rule 3.3 requires that attorneys disclose to the court "legal authority in the controlling jurisdiction known to the lawyer to be directly adverse to the position of the client and not disclosed by opposing counsel." Therefore, if an attorney discovers a case that is mandatory authority and directly contradicts one of his or her legal arguments, the attorney must disclose it to the court if the other side has not. The legal research and writing texts listed in Appendix D explain how to effectively distinguish such a case.

The Ohio Rules of Professional Conduct are included in Ohio annotated statutory codes, so the research methods described in Part III of this chapter are applicable. Because Ohio's rules are based upon the American Bar Association's Model Rules of Professional Conduct, the *Annotated Model Rules of Professional Conduct* may provide relevant cases from other jurisdictions. Remember that cases decided in other jurisdictions are merely persuasive authority.

VI. Finding Court Documents

When a new case is filed, a docket is created and the case is assigned a unique number, called a *docket number*. In Ohio, most courts use a combination of letters and numbers indicating the year the case was filed and the type of case it is. For example, docket number 2004-DR-0445 indicates that the case was filed in 2004 in a domestic relations court and was the 445th case of the year.

A *docket* lists all of the parties to the case, their counsel, and every document filed in the case, including decisions made by the court. An example of a docket appears in Figure 6-1. Types of court documents filed during a trial include complaints, answers, motions, and affidavits. Cases on appeal often produce briefs, oral argument transcripts, and opinions.

Figure 6-1. Sample Court Docket

Stark County Court of Common Pleas, Domestic Relations Division

Olivia Zhang v. Thomas Dubois
2004-DR-0445

Type of Action: Divorce
Judge: Maria Garcia
Case Status: Closed

02-14-2005	Judgment Entry.
02-14-2005	Decree of Divorce Granted — Granted to Plaintiff — each party to pay his or her own atty. fees and costs.
02-04-2005	Defendant's Motion to Compel — With Proof of Service Filed.
01-04-2005	Subpoena Issued — To Popov Restaurant Supply Attn Payroll Dept by Certified Mail.
10-20-2004	Notice of Serving Answers to Interrogatories and Production of Documents with Proof of Service.
09-07-2004	Judgment Entry: Overruled Objection.
08-24-2004	Notice of Filing Interrogatories and Request for Production of Documents Filed.
07-29-2004	Magistrate's Order Filed. Spousal Support $400.00 per month — Served in Court.
06-16-2004	Answer — Represented by Quinn Hoffman, Answer and Counterclaim filed by Thomas Dubois.
05-21-2004	Pre Trial set for 11-03-2004 at 11:15 AM.
05-21-2004	Complaint Filed — Represented by Vondra Roberts, Divorce without Children — Summons and Copies of Complaint, Affidavit, Motion for Restraining Order filed by Olivia Zhang.

Dockets and court documents are increasingly available online, although availability may be inconsistent. Federal appellate, district, and bankruptcy dockets and court documents may be available for a small fee via PACER.[8] Bloomberg Law, Lexis Advance, and WestlawNext have state and federal court dockets and court document databases. Ohio clerks of courts are increasingly making dockets available online, although the full text of the documents may not be available. The Supreme Court of Ohio's docket is available online and includes court documents.[9] To determine if a particular court's docket and court documents are available online, check the clerk of court's web page or contact the clerk of court. Although court documents are increasingly available online, many court documents are not and must be requested directly through the clerk of court.

Court documents for the U.S. Supreme Court from 1832 to 1978 are available online through Gale's Supreme Court Records and Briefs database, available in many academic law libraries. Lexis Advance and WestlawNext also offer more current collections of U.S. Supreme Court documents. Additionally, the Court website contains the Court's docket, links to merit briefs, and transcripts of oral arguments.[10] Many academic libraries also have this material available in microform, in addition to the oral argument transcripts. For the Supreme Court of Ohio, the Supreme Court of Ohio Law Library has the most comprehensive collection of records and briefs.

---

8. The address for PACER is at http://pacer.uscourts.gov.
9. The address is http://www.supremecourt.ohio.gov/.
10. The address is www.supremecourtus.gov.

Chapter 7

Researching Administrative Law

I. Administrative Law Generally

Administrative law is generated mainly by government agencies. Numerous agencies exist in both the federal and state governments. Although a few are established by the federal or state constitution, most agencies are created by statute. Most agencies fall under the executive branch of government, as shown in Figure 7-1; however, there are some independent agencies, such as the Ohio Civil Rights Commission, and legislative agencies, such as the Ohio Legislative Service Commission. As part of the executive branch of government, agencies are charged with implementing and applying the laws enacted by the legislature. To implement and apply the laws, agencies promulgate rules and issue decisions within their area of regulatory expertise.

Most agencies must have legislative authority to regulate a given area. In promulgating rules or adjudicating matters, agencies operate within the authority of an enabling statute and under the procedural requirements of an Administrative Procedure Act, or other similar statute. The enabling statute details what authority the legislature has given an agency and it can vary in scope from very broad to specific. When an agency acts beyond its enabling statutes, the actions (like regulations) may not be enforceable.

The federal government enacted the Administrative Procedure Act (APA)[1] to promote uniform operation of the numerous federal agencies. Ohio, like many other states, adopted its own version, known as the Ohio Administrative Procedure Act.[2] These types of statutes dictate the process that an agency follows in promulgating rules and issuing opinions.

---

1. 5 U.S.C. §§ 551–559 (2012).
2. Ohio Rev. Code Ann. §§ 119.01–119.13 (West 2002 & Supp. 2014).

Figure 7-1. Branches of Government

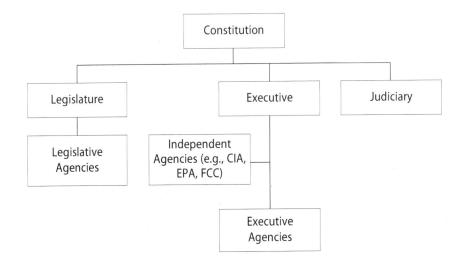

In Ohio, there are two types of agencies: Chapter 119 agencies and Section 111.15 agencies. Chapter 119 agencies fall under the procedures of the Ohio APA codified in Chapter 119; Section 111.15 agencies must meet the requirements of Ohio Revised Code § 111.15. The main difference between the two procedural requirements involves public notice: Chapter 119 agencies must provide public notice of rule making activity while Section 111.15 agencies do not.

II. Researching Administrative Rules and Regulations

Agencies promulgate rules (often referred to as *regulations*) to implement statutes. Often, statutes are general in their language. To apply or enforce a statute, agencies draft more detailed rules. Both the rules and the underlying statutes are primary authority and as such carry the force of law; given any discrepancy between the two, the statutes control. Table 7-1 provides an example of this relationship.

Table 7-1. Example of the Relationship Between a Statute and Rules

Statute

The Ohio General Assembly instructed the State Medical Board to adopt rules that define and establish requirements for blood and body fluid precautionary practices to be used during invasive procedures to reduce the risk of exposure to HIV and hepatitis. *See* Ohio Rev. Code Ann. § 4731.051 (West 2013).

Rules

In a series of rules, the State Medical Board established specific definitions and standards for hand washing, disinfection and sterilization, disposal of wastes, etc. *See* Ohio Admin. Code § 4731-17-01 to 4731-17-07 (2013).

Unlike in the federal system, Ohio agency rules are subject to legislative review. A legislative committee, the Joint Committee on Agency Rule Review (JCARR), reviews proposed rules for various issues. The JCARR also ensures that the agency has the authority to promulgate the rule and that the rule does not conflict with other rules or the legislative intent of the underlying statute.[3]

A. General Approaches to Researching Administrative Rules

Locating administrative rules can be challenging. Quite a few rules exist, both on the state and federal level. They often contain unfamiliar, technical language that can easily be missed by one unacquainted with the regulated area. Before searching a collection of administrative rules, it is often best to begin with other types of sources:

- Annotated statutory codes, such as *Baldwin's Ohio Revised Code Annotated* or the *United States Code Annotated*, often contain references to corresponding rules in the annotations.

- Secondary sources, such as practice treatises or legal encyclopedias, often contain references to applicable rules.

- The agency's website may provide an overview of the regulatory scheme, summaries or the full text of relevant statutes, regulations, and administrative decisions.

After consulting these other sources, you still might need to search for administrative rules directly.

---

3. For additional information, go to Members Only Briefs at www.lsc.ohio.gov/membersonly/ and click on "Overview of Administrative Rule-Making Procedure in Ohio."

Administrative rules are published in two types of sources: administrative registers and administrative codes (often referred to as regulatory codes). Administrative rules are first published in a chronological publication, often called a *register*. The rules are subsequently published in a codified publication, a regulatory *code*, in which the rules are arranged by agency and subject matter. When researching rules within a particular area, it is preferable to start with the codified collection of rules because it is arranged by subject matter and is often indexed.

However, chronological registers serve the important purpose of alerting the public to new regulatory activity that might not yet be included in the regulatory code, such as the adoption of new rules, amendments or repeals of existing rules, and the consideration of proposed rules. After you find an applicable rule, always update the regulatory code section using a chronological register or other regulation tracking database to check for any recent changes.

B. Researching Ohio Rules

1. Ohio Administrative Code

In Ohio, the regulatory code is called the Ohio Administrative Code (OAC).[4] It is similar to its federal counterpart, the Code of Federal Regulations (CFR), in that it contains rules arranged by agency and subject matter. Both sources are updated on an annual basis.

Baldwin's, part of West, publishes an annotated version of the OAC in print titled *Baldwin's Ohio Administrative Code Annotated*. The annotated version includes references to applicable court opinions and agency decisions as well as a very useful index. The annotated OAC is also available on Lexis Advance and WestlawNext. The state provides a free online version of the OAC, but it is unannotated.[5] Figure 7-2 contains an example of an Ohio rule on the state's website.

Several useful pieces of information appear after the text of the rule:[6]

---

4. Naming conventions for state administrative codes and registers vary from state to state. If conducting research in another state, use Table 1 of the *Bluebook* or Appendix 1 of the *ALWD Guide* to determine the name of the particular state's regulatory code and register.

5. http://codes.ohio.gov/oac/.

6. The example in Figure 7-2 is from a free unannotated version of the Ohio Administrative Code. If you are using an annotated version of the code, on WestlawNext or in print, the statutory references will be listed in the annotations.

Figure 7-2. Example of an Ohio Rule in the Ohio Administrative Code

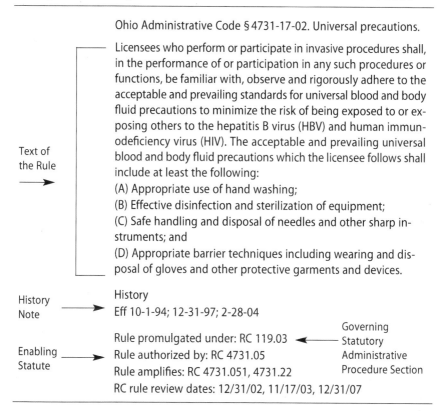

Ohio Administrative Code § 4731-17-02. Universal precautions.

Text of the Rule →

Licensees who perform or participate in invasive procedures shall, in the performance of or participation in any such procedures or functions, be familiar with, observe and rigorously adhere to the acceptable and prevailing standards for universal blood and body fluid precautions to minimize the risk of being exposed to or exposing others to the hepatitis B virus (HBV) and human immunodeficiency virus (HIV). The acceptable and prevailing universal blood and body fluid precautions which the licensee follows shall include at least the following:
(A) Appropriate use of hand washing;
(B) Effective disinfection and sterilization of equipment;
(C) Safe handling and disposal of needles and other sharp instruments; and
(D) Appropriate barrier techniques including wearing and disposal of gloves and other protective garments and devices.

History Note →

History
Eff 10-1-94; 12-31-97; 2-28-04

Enabling Statute →

Rule promulgated under: RC 119.03 ← Governing Statutory Administrative Procedure Section
Rule authorized by: RC 4731.05
Rule amplifies: RC 4731.051, 4731.22
RC rule review dates: 12/31/02, 11/17/03, 12/31/07

Source: Ohio Administrative Code, http://codes.ohio.gov/oac/4731-17.

- The history note lists changes made to the section and the effective date of those changes; in Figure 7-2, the rule was initially promulgated in 1994 and subsequently amended two times, once in 1997 and again in 2004.[7]

- Reference to the governing statutory administrative procedure section, which in Figure 7-2 is Chapter 119 of the Ohio Revised Code.

- References to the enabling statute authorizing the agency to issue rules, which in Figure 7-2 is Ohio Revised Code § 4731.05.

- References to statutory sections that the rule expands upon or amplifies, which in Figure 7-2 is Ohio Revised Code § 4731, subsections 051 and 22.

---

7. To see the text of the changes, you must look up the rule amendments by date in a chronological publication of Ohio rules, such as the *Ohio Monthly Record*.

2. *Ohio Monthly Record* and the *Register of Ohio*

Ohio has two publications covering regulatory activity. Each publication is useful for certain purposes.

The older publication is Baldwin's *Ohio Monthly Record*, which updates *Baldwin's Ohio Administrative Code Annotated.* Published since the 1970s, the *Ohio Monthly Record* is a print-only publication that publishes new and amended rules, in addition to giving public notice of repealed rules and proposed rules, on a monthly basis. Since it is published only monthly, it is not an ideal source to check for new regulatory activity. However, since it has been in publication since the 1970s, it is useful for researching past changes to rules.

The *Register of Ohio*, which began in 2000, is an online-only publication of the Ohio Legislative Service Commission and includes new and amended rules as well as proposed and repealed rules.[8] Although the *Register of Ohio* is updated weekly, rules are deleted from the database based upon a purgation schedule established by the Legislative Service Commission.[9] Given the purgation schedule, the *Register of Ohio* may not be useful for tracking past changes to rules. However, since the *Register of Ohio* is frequently updated, it is an invaluable source for checking for new rules or recent changes to existing rules.

3. Updating Ohio Rules

After finding an applicable rule in the OAC, check for any subsequent changes. There are several ways to update rules found in the OAC.

1. The *Register of Ohio*, as mentioned above, is a freely available source that you can search by agency or rule number for new, amended, or repealed rules.

2. Regulatory tracking databases available on both Lexis Advance and WestlawNext contain updated regulatory information.

3. KeyCite on WestlawNext covers Ohio rules. (But a note of caution: the KeyCite flags do not appear with Ohio rules; it is necessary to review the Citing References section of the KeyCite report).

Remember to always update the primary sources found in the legal research process.

---

8. It is available at http://www.registerofohio.state.oh.us.

9. For the *Register of Ohio*'s purgation schedule, see www.registerofohio.state.oh.us/jsps/public/pubPpurg.jsp. The "Register of Ohio" database on Lexis Advance is not purged.

C. Researching Federal Regulations

1. *Code of Federal Regulations*

In the federal system, administrative rules are referred to as *regulations*. Federal regulations are codified in the Code of Federal Regulations (CFR). Like the Ohio Administrative Code, the CFR arranges the regulations by agency and subject. The CFR is broken down into 50 titles that represent different areas of regulation (e.g., Title 7 covers agriculture, Title 42 covers public health). Often, the CFR and United States Code (USC) titles overlap (e.g., both Title 42 of both the CFR and the USC cover public health), but not always. Figure 7-3 shows a sample regulation from the CFR.

Figure 7-3. Sample Federal Regulation in the CFR

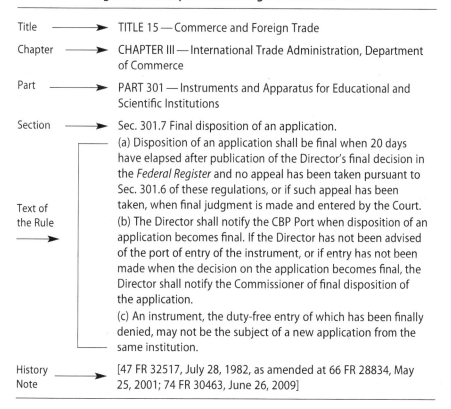

Title	TITLE 15 — Commerce and Foreign Trade
Chapter	CHAPTER III — International Trade Administration, Department of Commerce
Part	PART 301 — Instruments and Apparatus for Educational and Scientific Institutions
Section	Sec. 301.7 Final disposition of an application.
	(a) Disposition of an application shall be final when 20 days have elapsed after publication of the Director's final decision in the *Federal Register* and no appeal has been taken pursuant to Sec. 301.6 of these regulations, or if such appeal has been taken, when final judgment is made and entered by the Court.
Text of the Rule	(b) The Director shall notify the CBP Port when disposition of an application becomes final. If the Director has not been advised of the port of entry of the instrument, or if entry has not been made when the decision on the application becomes final, the Director shall notify the Commissioner of final disposition of the application.
	(c) An instrument, the duty-free entry of which has been finally denied, may not be the subject of a new application from the same institution.
History Note	[47 FR 32517, July 28, 1982, as amended at 66 FR 28834, May 25, 2001; 74 FR 30463, June 26, 2009]

Source: 15 C.F.R. § 301.7 (2014), available at www.gpo.gov/fdsys/.

Each title of the CFR is updated annually, on a staggered schedule. An index accompanies the print version of the *Code of Federal Regulations*. However, a more comprehensive index, entitled *West's Code of Federal Regulations General Index*, might be more helpful. Most academic libraries carry *West's General Index*.

The CFR is also available electronically from several sources. It is on both Lexis Advance and WestlawNext.[10] In addition, two versions are freely available through FDsys: the traditional CFR[11] and the Electronic Code of Federal Regulations (E-CFR).[12] The E-CFR is unique in that it is updated daily. HeinOnline provides retrospective access to the CFR back to its inception in 1938.

Like the Ohio Administrative Code, the CFR contains the text of a given regulation followed by a history note. The history note gives the date the regulation was originally issued or amended and the reference to the volume and page number of the *Federal Register* (FR) where the regulation appeared. In Figure 7-3, the history note indicates that the regulation was originally promulgated on July 28, 1982, and appears in volume 47, page 32,517 of the FR; it was subsequently amended on May 25, 2001, and the amendment appears in volume 66, page 28,834 of the FR. The reference to the enabling statute appears at the beginning of the chapter in the official versions of the CFR. In the Lexis Advance and WestlawNext versions, the authority note appears just after the source note. The authority note lists all of the enabling statutes while the source note shows all of the regulations that enacted and amended the code section over time.

2. *Federal Register*

Similar in function to the *Ohio Monthly Record* and the *Register of Ohio*, the *Federal Register* serves to notify the public of new regulatory activity. Published every business day, the *Federal Register* contains new or amended regulations in addition to proposed regulations and other types of public notices. Figure 7-4 provides an excerpt from the table of contents of an issue of the *Federal Register*, which demonstrates the different types of material it contains.

The *Federal Register* can also provide information that is helpful in interpreting the meaning of a regulation. The final rule often contains a summary of what has happened during the rulemaking proceedings. The proposed rule language is cited and the enabling legislation is identified. The agency often summarizes

---

10. The version of the CFR on WestlawNext is now annotated, including references to notes of decisions, and also includes an index.

11. The annual print edition of the CFR is preserved on FDsys, www.gpo.gov/fdsys. Access it by selecting the "Code of Federal Regulations" in the "Browse" section.

12. The E-CFR is available at http://ecfr.gpoaccess.gov.

comments on the proposed rule made by the public and those who may be affected by the proposed rule and then explains how the rule was changed as a result or defends its decision not to change the rule. This information from the agency can be very helpful not only in understanding the regulations, but in eliminating potential arguments about what the regulations mean.

Throughout the rulemaking process, the agency demonstrates its compliance with the Administrative Procedure Act and other procedural requirements to ensure that the rule will withstand a challenge to its validity.

Figure 7-4. Excerpt from the *Federal Register* Table of Contents

---

Contents   *Federal Register*
                                                          Vol. 80, No. 84
                                                          Friday, May 1, 2015

****

Coast Guard
RULES
Drawbridge Operations:
  Annisquam River and Blynman Canal, Gloucester, MA, 24814–24816
Safety Zones:
  Floating Construction Platform, Chicago River, Chicago, IL, 24816–24819

****

Centers for Medicare & Medicaid Services
PROPOSED RULES
Medicare Program:
  Inpatient Psychiatric Facilities Prospective Payment System, Update for Fiscal
  Year Beginning October 1, 2015 (FY 2016), 25012–25065
NOTICES
Agency Information Collection Activities; Proposals, Submissions, and
Approvals, 24934–24936

****

Federal Labor Relations Authority
RULES
Debt-Collection Regulations, 24779–24789

****

Federal Trade Commission
NOTICES
Proposed Consent Orders:
  Nomi Technologies, Inc., 24923–24929

Source: 80 Fed. Reg. (May 1, 2015), available at www.gpo.gov/fdsys/.

The *Federal Register* is freely available through FDsys from 1994 to the present. It is also available on Lexis Advance and WestlawNext. HeinOnline provides access to the *Federal Register* from volume 1 in 1936.

3. Updating Federal Regulations

After locating the applicable regulation in the CFR, next look for any subsequent changes to the regulation occurring since the CFR was last updated. There are several different ways to update a federal regulation:

- Check the regulation on the E-CFR, since it is updated frequently.
- KeyCite the regulation on WestlawNext, which covers federal regulations.
- Search the full text of the *Federal Register* online for references to the regulation.
- Search a federal regulation tracking database on Lexis Advance or WestlawNext.

Although the names of the specific sources differ, the underlying process for updating federal regulations is similar to the process used for Ohio administrative rules: use an up-to-date administrative register, KeyCite, or regulation tracking database to check for possible changes not yet included in the regulatory code.

III. Researching Administrative Decisions

In addition to promulgating rules, agencies also issue decisions or opinions. There are two basic types of agency decisions. First, similar to a court, an agency may decide disputes. As examples, a company may appeal the Federal Communication Commission's denial of a broadcast license or an individual may appeal an Ohio State Employee Retirement Board's denial of benefits. Second, many agencies provide advisory opinions to other government entities on legal issues. For example, the Ohio Attorney General may issue an opinion on the legality of a proposed government action.

A. Accessing Agency Decisions

The publication of both state and federal agency decisions is inconsistent. Some agency decisions are published in reporters, similar to case reporters, such as opinions of the Ohio Attorney General or the Federal Communications Commission. Conversely, many agency opinions are not formally published and consequently can be difficult to identify or obtain. However, a growing number of agency opinions are available online from Lexis Advance and WestlawNext. HeinOnline offers both a State Attorney General Reports and Opinions library and a U.S. Federal Agency Decisions library. Additionally, many agencies are making their decisions available on their respective websites. For example, Ohio Attorney General opinions from 1993 to present are available from the Ohio Attorney General's website.[13] The University of Virginia's Government Documents Library maintains a list of federal agency decisions freely available online.[14]

B. Updating Agency Decisions

Many formally published federal agency decisions can be KeyCited on WestlawNext or Shepardized on Lexis Advance. Unfortunately, Ohio agency decisions cannot be KeyCited or Shepardized. For a federal or state agency decision that cannot be KeyCited or Shepardized, an alternative approach is to search the full text of the relevant case law, agency decision, or statutory database to check for the decision's status and citing references.

IV. Citing Administrative Rules and Decisions

A. Rules and Regulations

If a regulation is in the regulatory code, such as the OAC or the CFR, then cite to that source. Citation to rules and regulations are covered by Rule 14.2 in the *Bluebook* and by Rules 18.1–18.2 (federal material) and 18.13 (state material) in the *ALWD Guide*. The *Ohio Manual of Citations* addresses rules on page 19. See Table 7-2 for an example of regulation citation.

If the regulation is too new to be in the regulatory code, then cite to the administrative register, such as the *Federal Register* or *Register of Ohio*. Citation to administrative registers is covered by Rule 14.2 in the *Bluebook* and Rules 18.3–18.4 (federal material) and 18.4 (state material) in the *ALWD Guide*. The *Ohio Manual of Citations* addresses administrative registers on pages 49 through 50.

---

13. At the general website, www.ohioattorneygeneral.gov, look for a link to "Formal Opinions," under the heading "State & Local Government."

14. This guide is available at http://guides.lib.virginia.edu/administrative_decisions.

Table 7-2. Regulation Citation Example

Citation Method	Examples	Source
ALWD Guide	Ohio Admin. Code 109:4-3-09 (2012). 29 C.F.R. § 101.18(a) (2014).	Rules 18.5 and 18.1
Bluebook	Ohio Admin. Code 109:4-3-09 (2012). 29 C.F.R. § 101.18(a) (2014).	Rule 14.2, Table T1, and Bluepages 14
Ohio Manual of Citations	Ohio Adm.Code 109:4-3-09. 29 C.F.R. 101.18(a).	Rule 4.4 and 4.5

B. Agency Decisions

Citing administrative agency decisions is similar to citing cases. Agency decisions are covered by Rule 14.3 in the *Bluebook* and Rule 18.5 (federal material) and Rule 18.15 (state material) in the *ALWD Guide*. The *Ohio Manual of Citations* covers administrative decisions on pages 18 through 19.

Chapter 8

Researching Local Law

I. Local Law Generally

Local law consists primarily of municipal ordinances and resolutions. *Ordinances* are permanent enactments, while *resolutions* tend to be temporary.

Municipalities, which are technically municipal corporations, include both cities and villages.[1] Municipalities are given authority to govern certain matters under the Ohio Constitution.[2] Municipal ordinances typically cover zoning, police, traffic, noise, and health standards for stores and restaurants. They are often organized by subject matter in municipal codes. An example of a municipal ordinance is provided in Figure 8-1.

In addition to municipalities, townships and counties may enact resolutions. Compared to municipalities, townships have similar, but much more limited home rule authority as dictated in Chapter 504 of the Ohio Revised Code. Counties are considered part of the state government and enact only temporary resolutions.[3]

Several secondary sources further explain the Ohio local government structure. *Baldwin's Ohio Practice* series on Local Government Law consists of three volumes: *County*, *Township*, and *Municipality*. This series is available on West-lawNext. Additionally, *Ohio Jurisprudence 3d* covers local law under the topic "Counties, Townships and Municipalities." Two general treatises, not specific

---

1. Cities have a population greater than 5,000; villages have fewer than 5,000. Ohio Const. art. XVIII, § 3.

2. Ohio Const. art. XVIII, § 3.

3. Ohio Const. art. X, § 1. The exception is Summit County, the only Ohio county that has passed the necessary charter under Ohio Constitution Article X, § 3, to exercise self-government.

Figure 8-1. Sample Municipal Ordinance

PART TWO — HEALTH CODE
Title I — Nuisances And General Provisions
Chapter 203 — Nuisance Abatement

203.01 Investigations; Remedial Measures
The Commissioner of Environmental Health or any authorized City officer or employee, upon complaint or information of the existence of any condition or thing which amounts to a nuisance which may affect or endanger the life, health or senses of the inhabitants of the City, shall investigate and take such measures as may be necessary to cause the abatement of any nuisance found to exist, by or at the expense of the person in charge or responsible therefor, or otherwise if circumstances so require.

(Ord. No. 511-76. Passed 6-14-76, eff. 6-18-76)

Source: City of Cleveland Code.

to the jurisdiction of Ohio, cover municipal corporations: *Law of Municipal Corporations* and *Local Government Law*. Both are available on WestlawNext.

II. Finding Municipal Codes

Municipal codes are not consistently available on Lexis Advance or WestlawNext. Lexis Advance currently contains five Ohio municipal codes: Akron, Athens, Cincinnati, Columbus, and Dayton. WestlawNext currently has no Ohio municipal codes; it actually has only one municipal code: New York City. Although Lexis Advance and WestlawNext provide limited coverage of municipal codes, the codes may be available online through the specific municipality's website or through one of the major commercial municipal code publisher's website. See Table 8-1 for a list of major municipal code publishers in Ohio.

Table 8-1. Commercial Publishers of Municipal Codes

Publisher	URL
Walter Drane / Conway Greene Co.	www.conwaygreene.com
Municode	www.municode.com
American Legal Publishing	www.amlegal.com

If an ordinance is unavailable online, the municipality's public library may have a copy in its collection. Otherwise, it will be necessary to contact the municipality's office to request a copy of a municipal ordinance.

III. Updating Municipal Codes

There are no uniform tools for updating a municipal code section. To check the currency of a municipal ordinance, check with the municipality.

IV. Citing Municipal Codes

Table 8-2 provides citation examples and references to relevant rules for citing municipal codes.

Table 8-2. Municipal Code Citation

Citation Method	Example	Source
ALWD Guide	Cleveland, Ohio, Codified Ordinances § 693.07 (2014).	Rule 17.1
Bluebook	Cleveland, Ohio, Codified Ordinances § 693.07 (2014).	Rule 12.9.2
Ohio Manual of Citations	Cleveland Codified Ordinances 693.07.	Rule 3.2

Chapter 9

Researching Secondary Sources

I. Secondary Sources Generally

Legal sources are broken down into two main categories: primary sources and secondary sources. *Primary sources* are the statutes, cases, rules, regulations, and municipal codes that comprise the law. Unlike primary sources, secondary sources are not the law. *Secondary sources* consist of the broad category of legal resources that help locate, explain, and analyze the law.

The first part of this chapter discusses the most commonly used types of secondary sources, such as legal encyclopedias, treatises, formbooks, and legal periodicals. The second part addresses more general secondary sources, including *American Law Reports*, Restatements, and uniform laws and model acts.

II. Legal Encyclopedias

Legal encyclopedias cover a broad range of legal issues. Arranged alphabetically by topic, they provide a brief overview of a legal issue accompanied by references to applicable primary sources. Because of their breadth of coverage, legal encyclopedias are often a good place to start in researching a legal issue.

There are two types of legal encyclopedias: national and state. National legal encyclopedias, namely *American Jurisprudence 2d* (called "Am Jur") and *Corpus Juris Secundum* (called "CJS"), attempt to cover all U.S. state and federal law. State legal encyclopedias focus on the law of a particular state. Although encyclopedias are not available for every state, there is a legal encyclopedia covering Ohio entitled *Ohio Jurisprudence 3d* (called "OJur").

Ohio Jurisprudence 3d divides the law into 400 topics, beginning with the topic "Abandonment" and concluding with the topic "Workers' Compensation." Figure 9-1 provides a modified excerpt from *Ohio Jurisprudence 3d*.

Figure 9-1. Excerpt from *Ohio Jurisprudence 3d*

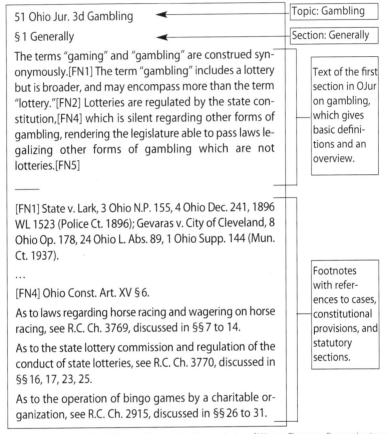

51 Ohio Jur. 3d Gambling ◄——————— Topic: Gambling

§ 1 Generally ◄——————— Section: Generally

The terms "gaming" and "gambling" are construed synonymously.[FN1] The term "gambling" includes a lottery but is broader, and may encompass more than the term "lottery."[FN2] Lotteries are regulated by the state constitution,[FN4] which is silent regarding other forms of gambling, rendering the legislature able to pass laws legalizing other forms of gambling which are not lotteries.[FN5]

Text of the first section in OJur on gambling, which gives basic definitions and an overview.

[FN1] State v. Lark, 3 Ohio N.P. 155, 4 Ohio Dec. 241, 1896 WL 1523 (Police Ct. 1896); Gevaras v. City of Cleveland, 8 Ohio Op. 178, 24 Ohio L. Abs. 89, 1 Ohio Supp. 144 (Mun. Ct. 1937).

…

[FN4] Ohio Const. Art. XV § 6.

As to laws regarding horse racing and wagering on horse racing, see R.C. Ch. 3769, discussed in §§ 7 to 14.

As to the state lottery commission and regulation of the conduct of state lotteries, see R.C. Ch. 3770, discussed in §§ 16, 17, 23, 25.

As to the operation of bingo games by a charitable organization, see R.C. Ch. 2915, discussed in §§ 26 to 31.

Footnotes with references to cases, constitutional provisions, and statutory sections.

American Jurisprudence 2d and *Ohio Jurisprudence 3d* are available on both Lexis Advance and WestlawNext. *Corpus Juris Secundum* is available only on WestlawNext. They are browsable and searchable on both systems.

To use the print version of *Ohio Jurisprudence 3d*, start with one of the following tools located at the end of the set:

• General Index volumes (indicating where a legal issue is covered in *Ohio Jurisprudence 3d*)

• Words & Phrases volumes (listing the cases where a word or phrase has been judicially defined)

• Tables of Laws and Rules (indicating which part of *Ohio Jurisprudence 3d* covers a given section of the Ohio Revised Code and the Ohio Administrative Code)

- Table of Cases (indicating where a given case is covered in *Ohio Jurisprudence 3d*).

To use legal encyclopedias online, it is best to do a simple search or browse the table of contents. Once you have found and read a relevant section, be sure to browse nearby sections or the table of contents to be sure that you do not miss other relevant sections.

When using the print version, be sure to check the pocket parts and supplements for updates to the material in the bound volumes.

III. Practice Treatises

Practitioners benefit from a broad collection of Ohio practice treatises that focus on specific practice areas, such as domestic relations law. Many of the Ohio practice treatises discussed below also include useful forms and checklists for drafting documents and courtroom procedure. Given their often in-depth treatment of a given practice area, practice treatises offer an effective starting point for researching a legal issue.

One of the major series of Ohio practice treatises is *Baldwin's Ohio Practice* series. Titles in the series are listed in Table 9-1. In addition to practice treatises, Baldwin's also publishes numerous handbooks that typically provide applicable statutory and regulatory code sections supplemented with some editorial commentary. Published by West, both treatises and handbooks are available on WestlawNext.

Table 9-1. List of *Baldwin's Ohio Practice* Treatises

Baldwin's Civil Practice
Baldwin's Ohio School Law
Business Organizations
Criminal Law
Domestic Relations Law
Elements of an Action
Evidence
Local Government Law (County, Municipal, and Township Laws)
Merrick-Rippner Probate Law
Real Estate Law
Tort Law

Anderson Publishing, owned by LexisNexis, also publishes several useful Ohio practice treatises. Some published titles are listed in Table 9-2.

Table 9-2. List of LexisNexis's Ohio Practice Treatises

Anderson's Ohio Civil Practice with Forms
Anderson's Ohio Corporation Law
Anderson's Ohio Family Law
Anderson's Ohio School Law Guide
Anderson's Ohio Securities Law and Practice
Employment in Ohio
Ohio Business Entities
Ohio Probate Practice and Procedure
Ohio Real Property Law and Practice
Weissenberger's Ohio Evidence Library

Additionally, LexisNexis offers many legal handbooks that contain the relevant statutory and regulatory code sections, supplemented with some commentary. These titles are also available on Lexis Advance.

The trick to using a treatise effectively both in print and online is to start with the index when one is available. It will hopefully provide a reference to the applicable section (note that references are sometimes given as chapter and section numbers rather than page numbers). If there is no index entry for your topic, try browsing the table of contents to locate the chapter that covers the topic. Unfortunately, online versions of many treatises do not contain an index. In that situation, it may be necessary to browse the table of contents or do a full-text search of the text of the treatise. However, WestlawNext makes indexes available for more sources than Bloomberg Law or Lexis Advance. When using print, always remember to check the pocket part or supplement of a print treatise for updated information.

IV. Forms

Legal practitioners draft a variety of documents, from contracts to court pleadings. *Form sets* provide samples of various types of legal documents that can be adapted for a specific situation. In addition to form sets, forms can often be found in practice treatises, as discussed above. It is important when using forms to make sure they comply with the law and court rules of the applicable jurisdiction.

Form sets can be divided into two categories: transactional form sets, and pleading and practice form sets. Transactional form sets cover business and personal contracts and transactions (e.g., sales of goods, prenuptial agreements, articles of incorporation). Pleading and practice form sets focus on litigation and court documents (e.g., motions, pleadings, interrogatories). Some form sets include both types of forms. The following provides a brief summary of the major sets of forms.

Using form sets is similar to using treatises: whether using a print or online version, start with the index when possible to find the location of the applicable form or alternatively browse the table of contents for the chapter covering the area (if looking for a sample will, browse through the chapter(s) covering wills). If using the index or browsing doesn't work, try a simple search. As with treatises, when using a print version remember to check the pocket part or supplement of a print form set for updated information.

A. Ohio Forms

Several form sets focus on Ohio. For transactional forms, the following sets are available:

- *Couse's Ohio Form Book* (available in print and on Lexis Advance)
- *Ohio Transaction Guide* (available in print and on Lexis Advance)
- *Ohio Forms: Legal and Business* (available in print and on WestlawNext).

For Ohio pleading and practice forms, several options are available:

- *Anderson's Civil Practice with Forms* (available in print and on Lexis Advance)
- *Ohio eforms: Ohio State & Federal Courts & Agencies* (available on WestlawNext)
- *Ohio Forms of Pleading and Practice* (available in print and on Lexis Advance).

WestlawNext's "Ohio Form Finder" helps locate Ohio-specific forms across practice areas. To search for Ohio-specific forms across practice areas and sources on Lexis Advance, simply select the jurisdiction "Ohio" and the category "Forms" in the search filters.

B. Federal Forms

For research focusing on federal practice, there are numerous pleading and practice sets, including:

- *Bender's Federal Forms* (available in print and on Lexis Advance)
- *West's Federal Forms* (available in print and on WestlawNext).

C. General Forms

In addition to the jurisdiction-specific form sets discussed above, there are several general form sets that are not specific to a given jurisdiction.

For general transactional forms, there are:

- *ALI-ABA Form Library* (available on Bloomberg Law)
- *American Jurisprudence Legal Forms 2d* (available in print and on Lexis Advance and WestlawNext)
- *Bloomberg BNA Sample Forms* (available on Bloomberg Law)
- *Current Legal Forms with Tax Analysis* (available in print and on Lexis Advance)
- *PLI Forms and Agreements* (available on Bloomberg Law)
- *West's Legal Forms* (available in print and on WestlawNext).

For a general set of pleading and practice forms, try *American Jurisprudence Pleading and Practice Forms Annotated* (available in print and on Lexis Advance and WestlawNext).

V. Law Journals, Legal Newsletters, and Blogs

Legal periodicals are excellent tools for keeping abreast of developments in a legal area. The two basic types of legal periodicals are law journals (or law reviews) and legal newsletters. Additionally, blogs have become an increasingly useful tool for learning about legal developments.

A. Law Journals

Law journal articles tend to be scholarly in nature. Most law schools publish at least one general law journal (e.g., *Ohio State Law Journal*); often times they publish additional specialty law reviews (e.g., *Ohio State Journal on Dispute Resolution*). A given issue may include articles by legal scholars, judges, or practitioners along with student-written articles (often referred to as notes or comments). There are also many commercially published law reviews that tend to focus on practice issues.

Numerous resources exist for finding law journal articles.

- Legal journal indexes: The *Index to Legal Periodicals* is available electronically through libraries that subscribe to it, including many academic law libraries. LegalTrac also is available online through many libraries and on both Lexis Advance and WestlawNext under the "Legal Resource Index."

- Full-text searching on commercial databases: Lexis Advance and WestlawNext generally have good coverage of law reviews from the early 1990s to the present. Bloomberg Law offers a growing collection of law reviews. You can search the full text of documents using terms-and-connectors or natural-language searching.

- HeinOnline: This online resource has a retrospective collection of law journals.

- The Legal Scholarship Network: This service has many published and forthcoming articles that can be downloaded, many of which are available free of charge.[1]

- Google Scholar: This search engine of scholarly literature is easy to use and free to search. Access to most of the articles is through your library or organization's subscriptions.

Law journal articles offer a good starting point for research. They often focus on a specific legal issue, providing an overview of the legal landscape and citations to primary and other secondary authority. Unlike legal encyclopedias or *American Law Reports* annotations (discussed later in this chapter), law review articles are often critical of the existing law and may suggest improvements. Like other secondary sources, law reviews contain citations to primary authority and, thus, may be a source for binding authority. Additionally, law journal articles might also carry persuasive authority. The factors influencing the persuasive value of an article include the reputation of the author, the reputation of the journal, and the age of the article. Once you find an on-point article, consider these criteria before relying on the article as persuasive authority.

B. Legal Newsletters

In addition to law journals, numerous legal newsletters are available. Although not scholarly like law journals, legal newsletters are excellent tools for keeping

---

1. The Legal Scholarship Network can be searched online at www.ssrn.com/en/index.cfm/lsn/.

abreast of legal developments in a given practice area. Practice-area newsletters and periodicals also may contain sample forms and other practice aids.

Bloomberg BNA publishes numerous newsletters covering various practice areas (e.g., banking, labor and employment law, tax). Each newsletter issue tracks developments in case law in addition to new legislation. BNA publications are available through Bloomberg Law and may be available at some academic law libraries.

Many legal newsletters are specific to Ohio legal practice. The Ohio State Bar Association (OSBA) publishes the *Ohio State Bar Association Report* (which reports on the activity of the OSBA) and the *Ohio Lawyer* (the OSBA's monthly magazine). Some newsletters focus on specific practice areas, such as *Ohio Code News*, the *Probate Law Journal of Ohio*, *Baldwin's Ohio School Law Journal*, *Domestic Relations Journal of Ohio*, and *Ohio Municipal Service*. Gongwer's *Ohio Report* and the *Hannah Report* cover the activity of the Ohio legislature. Additionally, the *Ohio Pending Opinion Report* summarizes pending Supreme Court of Ohio cases.

These newsletters may be found at academic law libraries in Ohio. Many of the newsletters are available online through Lexis Advance and WestlawNext.

C. Legal Blogs

Perhaps no category of secondary sources has grown more in recent years than legal blogs. Legal blogs, also known as "blawgs," cover topics ranging from cutting-edge developments in the substantive law to work-life balance. A legal blog may offer a good starting point for researching the law on a particular issue. However, the quality of blogs varies, and the researcher should evaluate the reliability of the source. Remember to confirm the accuracy of the law described in the blog post or other secondary source through original and independent legal research.

In addition to searching Google for possible legal blogs, legal blog directories provide lists of useful legal blogs. A few legal blog directories are listed below:

- *ABA Journal Blawg Directory*[2]
- *Justia Blawg Search*[3]
- *Law Library of Congress Legal Blawg Archive.*[4]

---

2. ABA Journal, *Blawg Directory*, http://www.abajournal.com/blawgs/.

3. Justia, *Blawg Search*, http://blawgsearch.justia.com/.

4. Law Library of Congress, *Legal Blawg Archive*, www.loc.gov/law/find/web-archive/legal-blawgs.php.

Additionally, many blogs focus specifically on Ohio law. A sampling of high-quality Ohio legal blogs is listed below:

- *Cleveland Law Library Weblog*[5]
- *Legally Speaking: Commenting on the Supreme Court of Ohio*[6]
- *Moritz Legal Information Blog*[7]
- *Sixth Circuit Appellate Blog.*[8]

Additionally, *Court News Ohio*[9] provides an RSS feed of recent decisions and court announcements (instructions for subscribing to the feed are available through the URL in footnote nine below).

VI. Jury Instructions

Jury instructions are an often-overlooked secondary source. Pattern jury instructions provide a useful tool for learning about an unfamiliar area of the law. While pattern jury instructions are intended for use by judges and attorneys when crafting instructions to be delivered to a jury before it deliberates, these instructions describe many claims and defenses in easy-to-understand language, which can be helpful at the beginning of researching a legal issue. Many instructions also are followed by commentary or annotations that cite to the primary authority that supports the pattern instruction. Thus, in addition to using jury instructions for background information on a legal area, the researcher can use jury instructions as a tool for locating relevant primary authority.

Ohio Jury Instructions (OJI) offer the most often-used and often-cited pattern instructions involving Ohio law. Written by the Jury Instructions Committee of the Ohio Judicial Conference, *OJI* contains pattern instructions for civil, criminal, and traffic cases. The Jury Instructions Committee both drafts pattern

---

5. *Cleveland Law Library Weblog*, http://suealtmeyer.typepad.com/cleveland_law_library_web/.

6. Marianna Brown Bettman, *Legally Speaking Ohio: Commenting on the Supreme Court of Ohio*, www.legallyspeakingohio.com/.

7. *Moritz Legal Information Blog*, http://moritzlegalinformation.blogspot.com/.

8. Squire Patton Boggs, *Sixth Circuit Appellate Blog*, www.sixthcircuitappellateblog.com/.

9. *Court News Ohio*, www.courtnewsohio.gov/.

instructions for new legislation and proposes updates to existing instructions. The print version of *OJI* is available in many Ohio law libraries and can be searched using its index and the table of contents. The full text of the *OJI* is also available on both Lexis Advance and WestlawNext.

In addition to *OJI*, the Ohio State Bar Association recently began publishing jury instructions. The *OSBA Jury Instructions* are more limited in scope than *OJI*, but they cover some issues not covered in *OJI*. The *OSBA Jury Instructions* are available through Casemaker, a legal database provided to OSBA members.

VII. General Secondary Sources

Although general in scope, numerous other secondary sources are helpful for researching Ohio legal issues.

A. *American Law Reports*

American Law Reports (called "ALR") consists of annotations, or articles, on specific legal issues.[10] An annotation generally provides a survey of how different jurisdictions approach a legal issue. Although annotations survey numerous jurisdictions, the table of jurisdictions at the beginning of an annotation lists cases and statutes by jurisdiction. Look for "Ohio" in that table, and you will find cases and statutes from Ohio that are relevant to the annotation's topic. A selected court opinion, which represents the issue discussed in the annotation, is published along with the annotation.

Early ALR volumes covered both state and federal topics, but federal issues were later moved to a dedicated series, *American Law Reports Federal* (ALR Fed). Thus, ALR 3d through ALR 6th series cover constitutional and state issues, while ALR Fed and ALR Fed 2d focus on federal and international topics. Table 9-3 gives examples of annotations found in the various series.

---

10. The use of the term "annotation" can be confusing. ALR annotations are distinct from annotations in annotated statutory codes. The annotations in statutory codes contain supplemental material, often cross-references to other code sections, notes of decisions, and references to secondary sources. ALR annotations are long articles that discuss a specific legal issue.

Table 9-3. Examples of *American Law Reports* Annotations

ALR 6th Series Annotation	*Lease Renewal Provisions as Violating Rule Against Perpetuities or Restraints Against Alienation*, 99 A.L.R. 6th 591 (2014).
ALR Fed 2d Series Annotation	*Discrimination on Basis of Person's Transgender or Transsexual Status as Violation of Federal Law*, 84 A.L.R. Fed 2d 1 (2014).

American Law Reports is available in print and also on Lexis Advance and WestlawNext. ALR may be searched by keyword online. In print, several search tools are available. If searching by topic, start with the index. ALR offers several indexes. The multi-volume ALR Index covers the 2d through 6th series and ALR Federal. There are two one-volume indexes, called Quick Indexes: the ALR Federal Quick Index (covering ALR Fed and Fed 2d) and the ALR Quick Index (covering ALR 3d through 6th series). The Quick Indexes are not as comprehensive as the main ALR Index.

In addition to using the index to search by topic, the ALR Digest may be used to search for annotations under a digest system.[11] When starting with a known case, the ALR Table of Cases references the ALR annotation that cites the case. When starting with a known federal or state statutory code section or a federal rule or regulatory code section, the Table of Laws, Rules and Regulations references the ALR annotation that cites the section or rule.

Once you find an on-point annotation, make sure it is up-to-date since ALR annotations may be supplemented or superseded. If using ALR 3d through 6th or ALR Fed in print, check the pocket part at the back of the annotation volume.[12] Also consult the Annotation History Table (located in the ALR Index volumes) for references to supplemented or superseded annotations from the ALR 2d through 6th series and ALR Fed.

B. Restatements and Principles — American Law Institute

Common law rules often vary across jurisdictions. The American Law Institute's (ALI) *Restatements* of the law attempt to condense the common law

---

11. In 2004, the ALR Digest adopted the West topic and key number system to classify cases.

12. Annotations from the first series of ALR are updated by the *Blue Books of Supplemental Decisions*. ALR 2d is updated by the Later Case Service.

into a uniform set of rules that reflect the current state of the law. The ALI's *Principles* contain the ALI's recommendation of what the law should be within a given legal area. Because of the painstaking drafting process and the respect within the legal community for the practitioners, judges, and scholars who serve as drafters, Restatements are among the most authoritative types of secondary sources. However, unless a Restatement or Principle is adopted by a jurisdiction, it is only persuasive authority.

There are currently 17 Restatement topics, which are listed in Table 9-4, and eight Principles, which are listed in Table 9-5. Each Restatement and Principle breaks down the law into a series of rules. Each rule is accompanied by comments that discuss the rule, illustrations that apply the rule to hypothetical situations, and summaries of cases that have applied the rule (if applicable).

Table 9-4. Restatement Topics

Agency	Property
Conflict of Laws	Restitution & Unjust Enrichment
Contracts	Security
Employment Law	Suretyship & Guaranty
Foreign Relations	Torts
Information Privacy Principles	Trusts
Judgments	Unfair Competition
Law of American Indians	U.S. Law of International Commercial Arbitration
Law of Consumer Contracts	

Table 9-5. Principles Subjects

Aggregate Litigation
Corporate Governance
Election Law: Resolution of Electronic Disputes
Family Dissolution: Analysis and Recommendations
Intellectual Property: Principles Governing Jurisdiction, Choice of Law, and
    Judgments in Transnational Disputes
Liability Insurance
Nonprofit Organizations
Software Contracts

Restatements and Principles are available in print and online through Lexis Advance, WestlawNext, and HeinOnline. If researching in print, start with the relevant Restatement or Principle subject name (e.g., Agency) and search the index for that set. As with research in most print sources, be sure to check the respective pocket parts for new case annotations. When using these sources online, select the appropriate subject (e.g., agency or torts) and browse the table of contents or search to find the relevant section. Once you find a relevant section, be sure to check nearby sections.

C. Uniform Laws and Model Acts

As Restatements promote uniformity within the common law, uniform laws try to achieve uniformity with state statutory law. As explained in Chapter 3, Part V.A., the National Conference of Commissioners on Uniform State Laws (NCCUSL) drafts many uniform laws that may be adopted by individual states. One of the most successful uniform laws is the Uniform Commercial Code, which has been adopted by all states. The NCCUSL designates a suggested law as a uniform law if it expects it to be widely adopted.

In addition to uniform laws, there are also model acts, which focus more on legal reform rather than uniformity. If the NCCUSL does not expect the law to be widely adopted, it uses the term model act. Many model acts are drafted by the American Law Institute as well as the NCCUSL. Unless these model or uniform acts are adopted by your jurisdiction, they are simply persuasive authority. If your jurisdiction has adopted the model or uniform act, these resources often provide supporting documents that explain the intent of the act and citations to cases interpreting the act as adopted in particular jurisdictions.

Uniform laws and model acts are available from several sources, including:

- *Uniform Laws Annotated* (ULA) (available in print and on WestlawNext). It includes a table of jurisdictions that have adopted a uniform law as well as commentary and notes about differences in enacted state laws.
- *Uniform Laws* (available on Bloomberg Law).
- *Uniform Law Commission Model Acts* (available on Lexis Advance).
- The National Conference of Commissioners on Uniform State Laws website.[13]
- Cornell's Legal Information Institute.[14]
- Martindale-Hubbell's *International Law Digest,* which is available on Lexis Advance.

---

13. *See* http://uniformlaws.org.
14. *See* www.law.cornell.edu.

VIII. Citing Secondary Sources

Different citation rules apply to the different types of secondary sources. Under the *Ohio Manual of Citations*[15] encyclopedias are covered on pages 55 to 56, law journal articles on pages 53 to 54, Restatements on page 51, and texts (including treatises) and dictionaries on pages 51 to 53.

Texts (including treatises) are covered by *Bluebook* Rule 15 (and Bluepages Rule B15) and *ALWD* Rule 20. Encyclopedias are also covered by *Bluebook* Rule 15, but the *ALWD Guide* treats them separately in Rule 22. Law journal articles fall under *Bluebook* Rule 16 (and Bluepages Rule B16) and *ALWD* Rule 21. Restatements and model codes follow *Bluebook* Rule 12.9.4 and *ALWD* Rule 23. Examples are provided in Table 9-6.

Table 9-6. Citation Examples for Secondary Sources

	AWLD Guide	Bluebook	*Ohio Manual of Citation*
Treatise	1 Angela G. Carlin, *Merrick-Rippner Probate Law* § 19.6 (7th ed. 2008).	1 Angela G. Carlin, *Merrick-Rippner Probate Law* § 19.6 (7th ed. 2008).	1 Carlin, *Merrick-Rippner Probate Law*, Section 19.6, 629 (7th Ed. 2008).
Legal encyclopedia	16 Ohio Jur. 3d *Condominiums & Co-operative Apartments* § 20 (2010).	16 Ohio Jur. 3d *Condominiums & Co-operative Apartments* § 20 (2010).	16 Ohio Jurisprudence 3d *Condominiums & Co-operative Apartments*, Section 20, at 27–28 (2010).
Restatement	Restatement (Second) of Contracts § 159 (1981).	Restatement (Second) of Contracts § 159 (1981).	1 Restatement of the Law 2d, Contracts, Misrepresentation, Section 159, at 426 (1981).
Law review article	John Quigley, *Ohio's Unique Rule on Burden of Persuasion for Self-Defense: Unraveling the Legislative and Judicial Tangle*, 20 U. Tol. L. Rev. 105 (1988).	John Quigley, *Ohio's Unique Rule on Burden of Persuasion for Self-Defense: Unraveling the Legislative and Judicial Tangle*, 20 U. Tol. L. Rev. 105 (1988).	John Quigley, *Ohio's Unique Rule on Burden of Persuasion for Self-Defense: Unraveling the Legislative and Judicial Tangle*, 20 U.Tol.L.Rev. 105 (1988).

---

15. *See* www.supremecourt.ohio.gov/ROD/manual.pdf.

Chapter 10

Researching Legislative History

I. Legislative History Generally

As proposed legislation works its way through the legislative process, the legislature generates various types of documents: alternate versions of and changes to the legislation, legislative reports, hearings, and debates on the value of the legislation. (See Figure 10-1.) Legislative history consists of these types of legislative materials produced during the enactment of a statute. While an enacted statute has the force of law, a statute's legislative history is not the law. The legislative history of a statute is at most persuasive authority. Even so, a statute's legislative history is often researched and cited in legal arguments.

Figure 10-1. Legislative Process

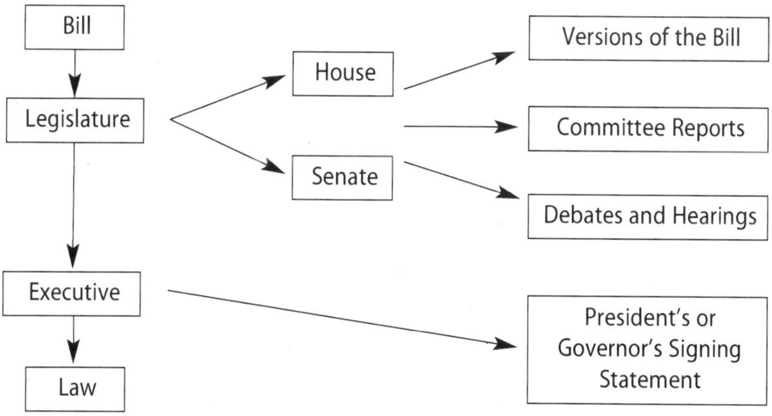

```
   ┌──────┐
   │ Bill │
   └──────┘
      │
      ▼
┌────────────┐        ┌────────┐         ┌─────────────────────────┐
│ Legislature│──────→ │ House  │────────→│  Versions of the Bill   │
└────────────┘   ╲    └────────┘    ╱    └─────────────────────────┘
      │           ╲                 
      │            ╲   ┌────────┐         ┌─────────────────────────┐
      │             ─→ │ Senate │────────→│   Committee Reports     │
      │                └────────┘         └─────────────────────────┘
      ▼                                   ┌─────────────────────────┐
┌────────────┐                            │  Debates and Hearings   │
│ Executive  │                            └─────────────────────────┘
└────────────┘──────────────────────────→┌─────────────────────────┐
      │                                   │   President's or        │
      ▼                                   │   Governor's Signing    │
┌────────────┐                            │   Statement             │
│    Law     │                            └─────────────────────────┘
└────────────┘
```

One of the primary uses of legislative history is in statutory interpretation. Often, statutory language can be unclear or ambiguous. For example, does the definition of a *motor vehicle* in section 4501.01 of the Ohio Revised Code include helicopters? To answer that question, the Supreme Court of Ohio in *Delli Bovi v. Pacific Indemnity*, 708 N.E.2d 693 (Ohio 1999), considered the law's legislative history. Specifically, the court pointed to one of the few available pieces of legislative history, the Summary of Enactments, which stated that the purpose of the law was to expand insurance coverage in automobile insurance policies. Based on that piece of legislative history, the court reasoned that the legislature only intended to include automobiles in the definition of motor vehicles.

Although attorneys may turn to the statute's legislative history to argue that the legislature intended a certain meaning, attitudes of judges and jurisdictions differ on the acceptability of legislative history in deciphering legislative intent. In Ohio, acceptance of legislative history in statutory construction is codified in Ohio Rev. Code Ann. § 1.49 (LexisNexis 2004). This section states that, if a statute is ambiguous, the court may consider legislative history in addition to several other factors.[1] Judicial acceptance of legislative history on the federal level is less uniform. Justices on the U.S. Supreme Court are split in opinion as to the usefulness of legislative history in establishing legislative intent.[2]

Another important use of legislative history documents is tracking pending legislation. This information is useful to researchers with an interest in potential new legislation or changes to existing legislation.

II. Overview of the Legislative Process

The basic legislative process is similar in the U.S. Congress and the Ohio General Assembly, although terminology and specific procedures may differ. The following section offers a brief overview of the general legislative process.

A. Bill Introduced

When members of the legislature see a need for a new law, they introduce proposed legislation in their respective legislative chambers (either the House or Senate). Proposed legislation is called a bill. For example, in response to

---

1. The factors listed in section 1.49 include "(A) The object sought to be attained; (B) The circumstances under which the statute was enacted; (C) The legislative history; (D) The common law or former statutory provisions, including laws upon the same or similar subjects; (E) The consequences of a particular construction; (F) The administrative construction of the statute."

2. 2A Norman J. Singer, *Statutes and Statutory Construction* § 48.02 (7th ed. 2014) (previously known as *Sutherland Statutory Construction*).

the growing incidence of identity theft in 2007, a member of the Ohio General Assembly introduced House Bill 46, which would modify existing law to allow consumers to freeze their credit reports. Many bills are introduced but few actually make it through the following process to become law.

B. Committee Activity

Once introduced, the bill is assigned to a corresponding House or Senate committee for consideration (e.g., U.S. Senate Committee on Armed Services or the House Committee on Education and Labor). The committee or a subcommittee may hold hearings on the subject of the bill. At committee hearings, members of the committee invite experts and other members of the public to testify on the given subject matter. For example, while considering the Ohio bill on credit reports, the House Committee on Financial Institutions, Security, and Real Estate held hearings to explore the need for new legislation; members of industry and consumer groups, and government officials spoke on the issue. After consideration of a bill and possible amendments, the committee "reports out" the bill to the chamber (the House or Senate), with a recommendation for action on the bill.

C. Floor Activity

If the committee favorably reports out the bill to the House or Senate, the chamber as a whole will then consider, possibly amend, and vote on passage of the bill. During legislative consideration, members of the respective chambers debate the merits of the bill. Amendments to the bill may be introduced by individual members and voted on by the respective chamber. If passed in one chamber, the bill is introduced in the other chamber and the process is repeated. A bicameral conference committee may be created to reconcile differences between House and Senate versions of a bill.

D. Executive Activity

Once the bill passes both chambers, it is sent to the executive (i.e., the President of the United States or the Governor of Ohio) for signature or veto. If vetoed, the bill must return to the legislature and pass each chamber by a super majority.[3]

---

3. U.S. Const. art. I, § 7 (requiring a two-thirds vote); Ohio Const. art. II, § 16 (requiring a three-fifths vote).

III. Federal Legislative History

Although the U.S. and Ohio legislative processes are similar, there are significant differences between the types of legislative history documents available at the federal and state levels. Given the different types of legislative history documents and the different sources for those documents, this chapter treats U.S. and Ohio legislative history separately. The chapter begins with federal legislative history because it has the widest selection of legislative history documents and provides a good point of comparison. Ohio legislative history is discussed in Part IV.

A. Types of Federal Legislative History Documents

The most common types of federal legislative history documents are bill amendments, committee hearings, committee reports, committee prints, congressional debates, and presidential signing statements. Additionally, the original and amended versions of a statute in the session laws reveal the changes made to a law over time.

Session Laws. Session laws contain the text of a bill as enacted. The *Statutes at Large* is the official publication of federal session laws. Along with the text of the statute, it contains limited references to legislative history sources. Session laws are also published in *United States Code Congressional and Administrative News* (USCCAN), along with some legislative history for select laws.

Bill Amendments. A bill is subject to numerous amendments (changes in the text) during its time in committee or when it is being considered by the Senate or House as a whole. A comparison of the changes in language may illustrate legislative intent.

Committee Hearings. Legislative committees often hold hearings to obtain testimony from experts or members of the public affected by a given issue. On the federal level, the full text of hearings is often, but not always, published.

Committee Reports. In reporting out a bill to the chamber, the U.S. House or Senate committee also issues a detailed legislative report, commonly referred to as a *committee report*. The committee report is one of the more useful types of legislative history. It typically includes the committee's recommendation on whether the bill should be enacted into law in addition to providing a summary, background information, and analysis of the legislation.

Committee Prints. The subject matter of committee prints varies widely, from research reports on specific topics to a compilation of laws. Committee prints are not authored by the committee but instead are requested by the committee for use in its work.

Congressional Record. The *Congressional Record* contains the record of proceedings in the U.S. House and Senate. Specifically, text of floor debates among members of the House and Senate can be found in the *Congressional Record*, along with the text of amendments offered during debates and member voting records.

Compilation of Presidential Documents. The *Compilation of Presidential Documents* contains presidential signing or veto statements, in addition to executive orders and proclamations.

B. Sources for Federal Legislative History Documents

Numerous sources are available for locating federal legislative history documents. If available for the statute at issue, the ideal source is a compiled legislative history. Available for selected major legislation, such as the Dodd-Frank Wall Street Reform and Consumer Protection Act or the Americans with Disabilities Act, a compiled legislative history contains all of the associated documents for the legislation. However, the majority of federal statutes do not have comprehensive compiled legislative histories, so it is often necessary to find the various individual legislative history publications. Fortunately, federal legislative history documents are relatively easy to access through a variety of sources. Many of the traditional sources for federal legislative history documents are fee-based, but an increasing amount of current material is freely available from government websites.

1. Fee-Based Sources Online

Many fee-based databases contain federal legislative history material. Lexis Advance provides compiled legislative histories of selected acts and bill tracking information back to 1989, but does not currently include legislative history documents in its version of the print or online version of the U.S. Code. WestlawNext offers a robust selection of federal legislative history publications. It includes compiled legislative histories, such as the large Government Accountability Office (GAO) federal legislative histories collection, as well as integration of legislative history documents into the annotations of its print and online versions of the U.S. Code. Additionally, HeinOnline contains compiled legislative histories and a growing collection of federal material. ProQuest Congressional and ProQuest Legislative Insight, available at most academic law libraries and many university libraries, are the most comprehensive sources of federal legislative history. Table 10-1 summarizes the types of legislative history documents available through the respective databases.

2. Free Sources Online

Two government websites, Congress.gov and FDsys, are the primary free sources for U.S. legislative information. Both sources provide good access to recent legislative material but do not cover material pre-dating the mid-1990s.

The Library of Congress created the Congress.gov website to provide free access to current and archived legislative information. It is an excellent source for legislative history research for more recent acts because it provides access to many of the important legislative history documents and links to even more on Government Publishing Office's FDsys database.

Congress.gov is searchable by bill number and keyword. For each bill, it includes summaries of the bill, as well as the bill sponsor, date of introduction, the latest action taken on the bill, any committee reports, and votes. Selecting one of the tabs along the bottom of the result screen provides more details.

3. Print Sources

If access to a fee-based source is unavailable or the law pre-dates the coverage on Congress.gov and FDsys, it may be necessary to use print sources. The following sources can often be found in many academic and public libraries, in print and/or microform.

- Compiled legislative histories
- Text of bills
- *Congressional Record*
- *Weekly Compilation of Presidential Documents*
- Congressional hearings (hearings from 1970 to present are available in the Congressional Information Service (CIS) Microfiche set; hearings prior to 1970 may be available in the CIS Unpublished and Published Hearings sets)
- Committee reports (reports from 1970 to present are available in the CIS Microfiche set; reports prior to 1970 to present are available in the U.S. Serial Set)
- USCCAN

Many academic libraries make their catalogs freely available online or through WorldCat and can be searched for a library's given holdings. Additionally, ProQuest and other companies have recently digitized many of their

Table 10-1. Sources for Online Legislative History

Database	Contents
Bloomberg Law	The "U.S. Congress" database includes bills (from 1993), committee reports (from 2007), selected committee testimony (from 2007), the *Congressional Record* (back to 1939), and roll call votes (from 2005).
Congress.gov	Information about bills (from 1973), full text of bills and amendments (from 1993 and 1995 respectively), committee reports (from 1995), and the *Congressional Record* (from 1995).
FDsys	Bills (from 1993), congressional documents (including committee prints) (from 1975), committee reports (from 1995), selected committee hearings (from 1985), and the *Congressional Record* (from 1994).
HeinOnline	The "U.S. Congressional Documents" library includes the *Congressional Record* (from its inception and its predecessors), select committee hearings (back to 1889), select Congressional Research Service (CRS) reports, and select committee prints (back to 1933). The "U.S. Federal Legislative History Library" includes the full text of selected compiled legislative histories as well as the "Sources of Compiled Legislative Histories" database.
Lexis Advance (Older content may currently be available in Lexis.com and may eventually be added to Lexis Advance.)	Includes committee reports (from 2000), bills (from 1989), the *Congressional Record* (from its inception and its predecessors), voting records (from 1987), and hearing transcripts (from 2007).
ProQuest Congressional	Bills, committee documents (including reports, prints, and hearings), unofficial committee hearing transcripts, the *Congressional Record* and its predecessors (all from 1789), and selected CRS reports (from 1916). Comprehensive compiled legislative histories for all enacted laws since 1970.
ProQuest Legislative Insight	Comprehensive compiled legislative history for selected enacted laws from 1789 to the present.
WestlawNext	Selected committee reports (from 1948), the *Congressional Record* (from 1985), unofficial transcripts of committee hearings (from 1997), and selected compiled legislative histories (from 1921).

historical collections, such as the Serial Set, committee hearings, and the *Congressional Record*. These databases might be available at some academic libraries. Finally, much of this material is increasingly available for free online, such as through Google Books.[4]

C. Finding Federal Legislative History Documents

To begin researching the legislative history of a federal statute, start by finding the public law number and *Statutes at Large* citation for the statute. Remember that the public law number is a unique number assigned to each Act. This will be in the history note of the *United States Code* section. (See Figure 10-2.)

Figure 10-2. History Note in *United States Code*

---

35 U.S.C. § 4. Restrictions on officers and employees as to interest in patents

Officers and employees of the Patent and Trademark Office shall be incapable, during the period of their appointments and for one year thereafter, of applying for a patent and of acquiring, directly or indirectly, except by inheritance or bequest, any patent or any right or interest in any patent, issued or to be issued by the Office. In patents applied for thereafter they shall not be entitled to any priority date earlier than one year after the termination of their appointment.

(July 19, 1952, c. 950, 66 Stat. 793; Jan. 2, 1975, Pub.L. 93-596, § 1, 88 Stat. 1949.)

History note: The original statute enacted in 1952 can be found in volume 66 of the *Statutes at Large*.

History note: The 1975 amendments can be found in volume 88 of the *Statutes at Large*.

If the statute was a major piece of legislation (e.g., Americans with Disabilities Act, Dodd-Frank Act), look for a compiled legislative history. Compiled legislative histories may be found in academic law libraries, on Lexis Advance, WestlawNext, or HeinOnline. HeinOnline's *Sources of Compiled Legislative History* serves as a finding aid. With the public law number, you can determine if a compiled legislative history exists in one of many databases or in print.

If there is no compiled legislative history, the next best source is either ProQuest Congressional or ProQuest Legislative Insight, since they provide com-

---

4. The address is http://books.google.com.

prehensive legislative information that can be easily searched for provisions relevant to a specific public law. As mentioned above, academic libraries may provide access to ProQuest Congressional and Legislative Insight. If using WestlawNext, pull up the statutory section in the USCA. Legislative history publications are located under the "History" tab. Under the history tab, the "Legislative History Materials" section contains a list of legislative history publications for each act that enacted or amended the statutory section. Many of the publications are followed by a hyperlinked citation, where the full text of the publication can be found. Unfortunately, there is currently no way to search multiple documents simultaneously. If the law is relatively current, try Congress.gov. Figure 10-3 is an example of the summary page for Public Law 113-4, the Violence Against Women Reauthorization Act of 2013.

Figure 10-3. Bill Summary on Congress.gov

Source: Congress.gov www.congress.gov/bill/113th-congress/senate-bill/47

D. Tracking Current Federal Legislation

Researching the current status of pending federal legislation is essential for keeping abreast of possible federal legislation impacting a specific practice area and alerting clients to new laws that may affect their interests. There are numerous online resources available to facilitate this process.

1. Using Congress.gov to Track Federal Legislation

As discussed above, the Library of Congress's Congress.gov website provides free access to current and archived legislative information. Using Congress.gov's bill reports is one of the best methods of tracking current federal legislation. The bill reports provide access to up-to-date information on bills, including the latest activities related to each bill. Because so much federal legislative history is available digitally, these running records often link directly to the full text of related documentation, such as committee reports, floor debate as published in the *Congressional Record*, amendments, and recorded votes. Congress.gov offers three types of email alerts: (1) the member alert provides an email notification when legislation is introduced by a particular member of Congress, (2) the legislation alert provides an email notification on activity related to a specific bill, such as a new summary, text, cosponsor, or action, and (3) the *Congressional Record* alert sends an email notification when a new issue of the *Congressional Record* is available.

2. Other Online Sources for Tracking Federal Legislation

Although Congress.gov is an excellent source for tracking federal legislation from 1995 to present, there are several other tools that provide similar information.

a. Govtrack.us

Use Govtrack.us to receive timely notifications via email or RSS of congressional actions on a bill as well as track actions of a member of Congress or the activity of a particular committee. It is possible to track documents containing specific keywords, that relate to an individual bill number, or that affect a specific U.S. Code section.

b. WestlawNext

WestlawNext's Federal Bill Tracking database includes summaries and the current status of pending federal legislation. Similar to Congress.gov, this database is updated daily. The "Bill Tracking: Historical" covers bills back to 2005. Alerts may be set up in both databases.

c. Lexis Advance

Lexis Advance includes bill tracking information in the "Congressional Bill Tracking" database. Historical bill tracking information is available for previous sessions of Congress back to 1989.

d. Bloomberg Law

Bills from the current Congress are available on Bloomberg Law, under the "Legislative & Regulatory" tab. Bills from previous Congresses are available back to 1993 in the "Legislative Materials" database. Alerts may also be set up within these databases.

IV. Ohio Legislative History

As in most other states, legislative history information in Ohio is relatively limited. Although the legislative process in Ohio mirrors the federal process, Ohio legislative history documents differ in many ways from their federal counterparts. For instance, Ohio does not have an equivalent to federal committee reports and committee hearing publications. Unlike the detailed legislative report authored by committees in the U.S. Congress, a committee report from the Ohio General Assembly is a yes or no recommendation given by the committee as the committee reports out the bill to the chamber as a whole. Also, there are no published transcripts of committee hearings or legislative debates in Ohio, although a few commercial services provide summaries of the hearings and debates.

A. Types of Ohio Legislative History Documents

Although Ohio does not have the identical types of legislative history documents available in federal legislative history research, other sources are available that aid in compiling the legislative history of an Ohio law.

Session Laws. The *Laws of Ohio* is the official publication of Ohio session laws, which allows the researcher to view a law as enacted and uncodified. The printed *Laws of Ohio* ceased in 2006; the Secretary of State publishes a certified version online.[5] Session laws may also be found in the commercial advanced legislative services, specifically *Baldwin's Ohio Legislative Service Annotated.*

---

5. This version is available at www.sos.state.oh.us/SOS/historicaldocuments/LawsofOhio.aspx.

Bill Amendments and Substitute Bills. As with federal legislation, the changes made to Ohio bills may illustrate legislative intent. If the changes to a bill are significant, then a substitute bill is introduced.

Legislative Service Commission (LSC) Bill Analysis. An LSC Bill Analysis summarizes how the bill would change existing law. The analysis is updated at different points in the legislative process. The analysis is a good source for obtaining an overview and background of the legislation.

Fiscal Note and Local Impact Statements. The fiscal note and local impact statements provide an estimate of revenue and expenditures associated with the proposed legislation.

Senate and House Journals. Similar to the federal *Congressional Record*, the Ohio Senate and House *Journals* provide a record of the proceedings in the Ohio Senate and House. However, the Ohio Senate and House *Journals* do not provide the same depth of information as the *Congressional Record*. The Ohio Senate and House *Journals* chronicle the procedural activity of the legislature and provide a record of votes and the text of amendments, but they do not print the verbatim text of debates.

Bulletin of the General Assembly and LSC Legislative Status Sheet. The Bulletin of the General Assembly lists the activity on each bill (i.e., when and to what committee the bill was assigned, any amendments, when the committee reported the bill, etc.). The status of current bills is available online through the LSC Legislative Status Sheet.[6]

Digest of Enactments. Organized by subject area, the Digest of Enactments provides a summary of all bills enacted in a given period. It began in 1997.

Bill Synopsis. There are three types of synopses: comparative bill synopsis, committee amendments synopsis, and conference committee synopsis. Each type of synopsis provides a summary of changes made to the bill by either a substitute bill or committee amendments.

B. Sources of Ohio Legislative History Documents

Numerous sources are available for finding the various types of Ohio legislative history documents. For relatively current laws, from the mid-1990s to present, legislative history information can be accessed online. For older statutes, it may be necessary to conduct research in print sources.

---

6. The address is www.lsc.ohio.gov/statusreport/.

1. Fee-Based and Free Sources Online

Several online sources provide access to Ohio legislative history information. In addition to the coverage on Lexis and Westlaw, two other subscription sources contain Ohio legislative history information: Gongwer News Service[7] and Hannah Capitol Connection.[8] Both services monitor Ohio legislative activity and provide good news coverage.

The Ohio General Assembly website[9] and the Ohio Legislative Service Commission are the primary sources for freely available legislative history information.

Table 10-2 compares the availability of Ohio legislative history documents on the respective free and fee-based databases. The beginning date of coverage is given in each column.

2. Print Sources

If unavailable online, many of the sources for Ohio legislative history can be found at the State Library of Ohio, the Supreme Court of Ohio Law Library, or one of the many county and academic libraries in Ohio (see Appendix C of this book). The Ohio History Connection houses the Ohio Bill Files, a comprehensive collection of available legislative history documents for each enacted bill.

C. Finding Ohio Legislative History Documents

To research the legislative history of an Ohio statute, begin by finding the enacted bill number of the statute at issue. It is in the history note of the Ohio Revised Code section. (See Figure 10-4.)

If the law was passed in 1989 or later and you have access to Hannah Capitol Connection, start there. In addition to the text of the enacted bill, Hannah provides comprehensive access to legislative history documents including summaries of committee meetings and hearings.

If access to Hannah is unavailable, and the law is from 2001 or later, use the Ohio General Assembly website to locate different versions of the bill, bill synopsis, and LSC bill analysis. Additionally, legislative history information may be available on either Lexis Advance or WestlawNext. Although its availability may be limited, Gongwer provides good news coverage of legislative activity.

---

7. Gongwer is available at www.gongwer-oh.com.

8. The address is www.rotundacollection.com.

9. *See* www.legislature.ohio.gov.

Table 10-2. Online Sources for Ohio Legislative History

	General Assembly	Ohio LSC	Westlaw-Next	Lexis Advance	Hannah Capitol Connection
Bills	122d (1997–98)	—	2005	1991	117th (1987–88)
LSC Bill Analysis	122d (1997–98)	122d (1997–98)	122d (1997–98)	Full coverage 2006; selected coverage 2002	119th (1991–92)
House Journals	125th (2003–04)	—	125th (2003–04)	—	—
Senate Journals	126th (2005–06)	—	126th (2005–06)	—	—
Governor's Message	—	—	2000	Full coverage 2006; selected coverage 2002	—
Committee Meetings and Hearings	—	—	—	Full coverage 2006; selected coverage 2002; summaries	125th (2003–04) summaries
Bill Synopsis	124th (2001–02)	124th (2001–02)	124th (2001–02)	Full coverage 2006; selected coverage 2002	—
Fiscal Note	122d (1997–98)	122d (1997–98)	—	Full coverage 2006; selected coverage 2002	—
Acts	122d (1997–98)	—	117th (1987–88)	119th (1991–92)	118th (1989–90)

If the law pre-dates the coverage of Lexis and Westlaw, research the legislative history in print. Locate an academic or public library in Ohio and ask a reference librarian for help in accessing the material.

D. Tracking Ohio Legislation

Researching potential changes to Ohio legislation is a common activity both to keep abreast of potential new legislation impacting a specific practice area or potentially impacting clients. Several online resources are available to facilitate this process.

Figure 10-4. History Note for Ohio Statute

Ohio Revised Code § 4109.11 Records to be kept

Every employer shall keep a time book or other written records which shall state the name, address, and occupation of each minor employed, the number of hours worked by such minor on each day of the week, the hours of beginning and ending work, the hours of beginning and ending meal periods, and the amount of wages paid each pay period to each minor. The director of commerce or the director's authorized representative shall have access to and the right to copy from the time book or records. Records shall be kept for a period of two years. No employer shall fail to keep such time book or records, or knowingly make false statements therein, or refuse to make the time book and records accessible, upon request, to the director or the director's authorized representative.

(1999 H 471, eff. 7-1-00; 1995 S 162, eff. 10-29-95; 1978 H 883, eff. 1-12-79)

History note: Most recent amendment in *Laws of Ohio* from 1999, enacted House Bill 471.

History note: Original statute was enacted in 1978 and is in the 1978 volume of *Laws of Ohio*, enacted House Bill 883.

Source: *Baldwin's Ohio Revised Code Annotated*. Reprinted with permission of West, A Thomson Reuters business.

1. Govtrack.us

This free service provides timely notification via email or RSS of newly proposed Ohio bills. Currently, it is not possible to track particular bills or topics.

2. WestlawNext

WestlawNext's Ohio Bill Tracking database includes summaries and the current status of pending legislation in the Ohio Legislature. This database is updated frequently. The Ohio Bill Tracking: Historical database covers bills back to 2005. Alerts may be set up to track a particular bill or topic.

3. Lexis Advance

Lexis Advance includes bill tracking information in the "Ohio Bill Tracking Reports" database. Historical bill tracking reports are available back to 1989. Alerts may be set up to track a particular bill or topic.

4. Hannah Capitol Connection

Hannah Capitol Connection, a subscription service, offers several tools for tracking Ohio legislation: (1) email alerts of pending legislation affecting specific sections of the Ohio Revised Code; (2) email alerts of any action taken on a particular bill, including the scheduling and rescheduling of committee meetings on a particular bill; and (3) email alerts of the introduction of new bills by specific legislators.

5. Gongwer

Gongwer, a subscription service, also provides several tools for tracking Ohio legislation. Email alerts are available to track bill activity, including when a bill is scheduled for a hearing, subject to any legislative action, or mentioned in a Gongwer news article. Email alerts can be set up to track committee activity, including when a committee meeting is scheduled or a meeting agenda is updated. Gongwer also offers the option of subscribing to one or more topics (e.g., agriculture or privacy) and receiving alerts when new bills on that topic are introduced. (These new bills may also be automatically added to an existing bill alert.)

V. Citing Legislative History Documents

Both the *Bluebook* and the *ALWD Guide* cover citation to legislative history documents. The *Bluebook* covers citation to federal and state legislative materials under Rule 13; the *ALWD Guide* covers citation to federal and state legislative history materials under Rule 15. The *Ohio Manual of Citations* does not specifically address citation to legislative history, so consult either the *Bluebook* or the *ALWD Guide* for citation form.

Table 10-3 shows a sample citation to Ohio House Bill 302, introduced on June 21, 2005, during the 126th General Assembly.

Table 10-3. Ohio Bill Citation Example

Citation Method	Example	Source
ALWD Guide	H.R. 302, 126th Gen. Assemb., Reg. Sess. (Ohio 2005).	Rule 15.13
Bluebook	H.R. 302, 126th Gen. Assemb., Reg. Sess. (Ohio 2005).	Rule 13.2 and Bluepages B13

Table 10-4 gives the citation format for federal House Report number 412, issued on October 29, 2007, during the 110th Congress.

Table 10-4. Federal House Report Citation Example

Citation Method	Example	Source
ALWD Guide	H.R. Rep. No. 110-412 (2007).	Rule 15.7
Bluebook	H.R. Rep. No. 110-412 (2007).	Rule 13.4 and Bluepages B13

Chapter 11

Research Strategies

I. Legal Research Process

This chapter illustrates the basic legal research process with a specific example. An overview of the basic legal research process from Chapter 1 is given in Table 11-1. As you become more comfortable with legal research, you will develop your own style and process. Until that point, you should follow this basic research process to ensure that you do not miss important mandatory authority.

Table 11-1. Overview of the Research Process

1. Determine the jurisdiction controlling the legal issue, if possible, and generate a list of *research terms*.

2. Consult *secondary sources* and practice aids, including treatises, legal encyclopedias, and law review articles, for an overview of the legal area and citations to primary authority.

3. Find controlling *constitutional provisions*, *statutes*, or administrative *rules* and read the relevant sections.

4. Use *case-finding tools*, such as headnotes or full-text searching, to locate any relevant cases. Read the cases.

5. *Update* your legal authorities to ensure they have not been repealed, reversed, modified, or otherwise changed.

6. *End* your research when you have no holes in your analysis and when you begin seeing the same authorities repeatedly. If you have used multiple methods in researching the legal issue, you are more likely to have found all of the relevant authorities.

II. Research Example

Imagine that you are working in a small firm in Columbus, Ohio. Your firm's client, Edward Lee, would like to have his new wife, Riya Patel-Lee, adopt his daughter, Campbell. Edward and his ex-wife (Campbell's mother), Sonya Moore, divorced seven years ago. Edward was awarded sole custody of Campbell. Sonya was awarded supervised visitations because of her substance abuse problems, but she has never taken advantage of the visitation opportunities. Sonya Moore has not spoken with or seen Campbell for three years, although she sends her a Christmas present every year. Sonya has not paid her court-ordered child support for four years. Campbell attends school in Worthington, Ohio, where Edward, Riya, Sonya, and Campbell live. Edward has hired your law firm to help with the adoption proceedings. You have been assigned to research the narrow issue of whether Sonya must consent to the adoption.

A. Generating Research Terms

Use the methods described in Chapter 1 to develop a list of search terms. Table 11-2 contains a list of possible search terms for this specific research issue using either a journalistic approach or the TARPP approach.

Table 11-2. Generating Research Terms

Journalistic Approach	
Who:	Parents (mother, father, step-mother), Child (daughter)
What:	Adoption, Abandonment, Support
How:	Consent
Why:	Abandonment, Substance Abuse
When:	Three years ago, Four years ago
Where:	Worthington, Ohio

TARPP Approach	
Things:	Child Support, Visitation
Actions:	Abandonment, No Contact, No Child Support, Adoption, Consent
Remedies:	Adoption
People:	Parents (mother, father, step-mother), and Child (daughter)
Places:	Worthington, Ohio

B. Consulting Secondary Sources

The next step in the research process is to consult secondary sources to obtain an overview of the subject matter, here adoption law, and to find references to primary sources such as statutes and cases.

General secondary sources, such as encyclopedias, will provide a broad overview of the subject. Browsing the index of *Ohio Jurisprudence 3d* (the Ohio legal encyclopedia) for the key terms turns up a large number of index entries on "Adoption of Children." Within that topic, the subtopic of "Consent" refers to "Family Law" sections 880 through 896. It is important to keep perusing the list even after finding one relevant entry. Continuing to browse the list turns up "Failure to communicate, consent not required" and "Failure to support, consent not required" listed as sections 894 and 895, respectively. These seem to be relevant sections.

An excerpt from section 895 of *Ohio Jurisprudence 3d*, Family Law, is reprinted in Figure 11-1. In addition to providing an overview of parental consent in adoption, it provides references to a West topic and key number, an Ohio statute, and a case that seems relevant to the issue of communication. Other sections provide similar guidance on the issues of consent and support.

Figure 11-1. *Ohio Jurisprudence 3d*, Family Law

---

47 Ohio Jur. 3d Family Law § 895

§ 894. What constitutes failure to support

West's Key Number Digest: West's Key Number Digest, Adoption 7.4(6)

In the statute specifying who need not consent to an adoption,[fn1] the failure to support proviso is an alternative to the failure to communicate proviso. A parent's consent is not required where the parent fails to provide support for one year, even if there has been some communication during the period. Thus, a natural parent's consent to an adoption is not required where that parent has failed without justifiable cause to provide support, even if that parent had some communication with the child during the same period and gave two Christmas presents to the child.[fn2]

As long as the parent makes some provision for the support of the child during the one year preceding the adoption petition, the statutory condition for dispensing with the parent's consent to an adoption is not satisfied even if the amounts are relatively small compared to the support obligation.[fn3]

Figure 11-1. *Ohio Jurisprudence 3d*, **Family Law,** *continued*

Illustrations:

... Likewise, evidence supported a finding that a mother failed to provide for the maintenance and support of her children, without justifiable cause, where the mother gave the son a computer game for his birthday and gave the children clothing and toys for Christmas, the maternal aunt and uncle requested $200 per week from the mother for support of the children, but the mother never paid any support to the aunt and uncle, and the mother was employed or able to seek employment during the applicable time period.[fn10]

Similarly, a father's purchase of toys and clothes for his daughter valued at about $133 is insufficient to fulfill his duty of support where the gifts to the child are not requested and they provide her no real value of support because she already has sufficient clothes and toys.[fn12]

Footnotes

1. R.C. 3107.07, discussed at § 889.

2. In re Adoption of Labo, 47 Ohio App. 3d 57, 546 N.E.2d 1384 (3d Dist. Shelby County 1988).

For a discussion of the failure to communicate proviso, see § 894.

3. Vecchi v. Thomas, 67 Ohio App. 3d 688, 588 N.E.2d 186 (2d Dist. Montgomery County 1990); In re Adoption of Salisbury, 5 Ohio App. 3d 65, 449 N.E.2d 519 (10th Dist. Franklin County 1982).

...

10. In re Adoption of James, 126 Ohio Misc. 2d 7, 2003-Ohio-5953, 799 N.E.2d 669 (C.P. 2003).

...

12. In re Adoption of Strawser, 36 Ohio App. 3d 232, 522 N.E.2d 1105 (10th Dist. Franklin County 1987).

Source: WestlawNext. Reprinted with permission of West, a Thomson Reuters business.

By finding and reading the *Ohio Jurisprudence 3d* section, you have identified several primary sources to further your research, especially Ohio Revised Code § 3107.07. Other secondary sources, which are discussed in Chapter 9, could provide more detailed information about the legal issues surrounding adoption or forms and checklists for drafting the documents that will eventually be filed in court.

C. Finding Statutes and Regulations

If the secondary source research does not produce citations to a statute, the next step is to begin searching for relevant statutory provisions directly in an annotated version of the Ohio Revised Code, Ohio's statutory code.

Using the search terms to search the Ohio Revised Code's index turns up the same code section referred to in *Ohio Jurisprudence 3d*. Under the topic of "Adoption," there is a subsection on consent. The subsection includes "unnecessary when, 3107.07," which leads to the same section as the research in *Ohio Jurisprudence 3d*. Encountering the same references in multiple sources generally signals that you are on the right track.

After examining the Ohio Revised Code, section 3107.07 looks promising. It provides:

Consent to adoption is not required of any of the following:

(A) A parent of a minor, [who] has failed without justifiable cause to provide more than de minimis contact with the minor or to provide for the maintenance and support of the minor as required by law or judicial decree for a period of at least one year immediately preceding either the filing of the adoption petition or the placement of the minor in the home of the petitioner.

Given the text of this statute alone, Sonya Moore's consent may not be necessary. However, the statute provides Sonya a defense of "justifiable cause." In other words Sonya Moore might claim that she had "justifiable cause" for not contacting or supporting Campbell, so her consent is necessary for the adoption.

This statutory research has revealed additional research questions. To fully answer your original question, you must now research what constitutes "justifiable cause," "more than de minimis contact," and "support." Next, using the table of contents, locate Chapter 3107's definitions section, 3107.01, and read that section to determine whether there is a statutory definition of these terms. If not, further research using these new research terms is necessary.

The annotations to this statutory section may provide citations to relevant regulations. Annotations are generally located just after the text of the statute in both the print and online versions. If you want to search for regulations in the Ohio Administrative Code, use the techniques described in Chapter 7.

D. Finding Cases

The next step in researching this legal problem is to find cases discussing and applying the concepts of "justifiable cause," "more than de minimis contact," and "support." Because the relevant statutory section has been identified, begin with the case annotations in the annotated statutory code. The case annotations list important cases that explain, construe, or apply the statute.

Case annotations are listed by topic. WestlawNext, for example, groups the cases annotating section 3107.01 into many categories including "In general," "Communication defined, failure to communicate," "Failure to communicate," "Failure to support," "'To provide more than de minimis' construed," and "Willful failure, failure to support."

If the secondary sources had not provided an overview of the legal issue, reviewing the cases listed in the "In general" category may provide that overview. Fortunately, each of the three issues that you identified as needing further research has a category. The remainder of this example will focus on the support issue. To complete the research, replicate the remaining steps for all of the legal issues, including justifiable cause, de minimis contact, and communication (called "contact" in the statute).

Skimming the case descriptions under "Willful failure, failure to support" provides many relevant cases. One case that looks promising is *In re Adoption of M.B.*, 131 Ohio St. 3d 186, 2012-Ohio-236, 963 N.E.2d 142. This Ohio Supreme Court case deals with whether regular Christmas and birthday gifts are enough to constitute maintenance and support, pursuant to section 3107.07(A), and trigger the requirement that parental consent is needed.

Reviewing this case on WestlawNext provides relevant topics and key numbers, which can be used to find additional relevant cases. Also, case citators, BCite, Shepard's or KeyCite, can be used to find later cases that apply the rule from *In re Adoption of M.B.*

E. Updating Authorities

Before relying on any case or using it in your legal analysis, update it with a citator to determine whether it is still good law. The KeyCite report on *In re Adoption of M.B.* indicates that there are several cases that have discussed or cited the case, but no negative treatment. Therefore, you may rely on this case and cite its rule concerning maintenance and support. Before using other cases, use the techniques described in Chapter 5 to update a case and to narrow long lists of citing cases by topic and jurisdiction.

You can also use the techniques in Chapter 5 to update statutes. Doing so ensures that the statute is still good law and that there is no pending legislation. In addition, a citator report for a statute can lead to more cases relevant to the issue.

F. Concluding Your Research

Before finishing any research project, make sure that you have thoroughly researched each legal issue and that the statutes and cases you have found are still "good law." End your research when you have no holes in your analysis and when you begin seeing the same authorities repeatedly. Using the same process for each legal research problem will ensure that your research is thorough.

Chapter 12

Legal Citation[1]

I. Introduction to Legal Citation

A legal document must convince a lawyer or judge reading it that its arguments were well researched and its analysis is well supported. Legal writers do this by providing references to the authorities used to develop that analysis and reach the conclusion. These references are called *legal citations*. In a legal document, every legal rule and every explanation of the law must be cited.

A. The Purpose of Legal Citation

A legal citation conveys several important pieces of information. First, it tells the reader where the cited authority is located so that the reader can find it. Second, it conveys the type of support the cited authority lends to the argument. Third, it briefly characterizes the weight of authority provided. Fourth, as part of a written document, it shows that the writer has been thorough and careful with research. Table 12-1 includes a citation to a case and explains the information provided.

---

[1]. Portions of this Chapter, especially those dealing with the *Bluebook*, are drawn from *Oregon Legal Research* and *North Carolina Legal Research* and are used with permission of the authors.

Table 12-1. Citation Example[2]

See Bd. of Educ., Cincinnati v. HEW, 396 F. Supp. 203 (S.D. Ohio 1975), *aff'd in part and rev'd in part on other grounds*, 532 F.2d 1070 (6th Cir. 1976).

- This case is located in volume 396, on page 203, of the *Federal Supplement*, which is abbreviated F. Supp.

- The signal *"See"* at the beginning of the citation tells the reader that this case implicitly supports the asserted proposition.

- The cited case is a federal district court case decided in 1975.

- The United States Court of Appeals for the Sixth Circuit decided an appeal of the cited case in 1976; it affirmed in part and reversed in part on other grounds.

Another important function of legal citation is to properly attribute the ideas, information, or language incorporated into a document to its original source, so as to avoid plagiarizing the original source. As defined by *Black's Law Dictionary*, plagiarism is "[t]he deliberate and knowing presentation of another person's original ideas or creative expression as one's own."[3] With proper citation, cited works are credited to the authors, avoiding unintentional plagiarism.

Legal researchers need to be able to read citations and quickly extract vital information from the citations. New legal researchers should memorize the information abbreviations in Table 12-2 so that they can quickly determine the precedential authority of the cited material and decide how to prioritize the pursuit of many citations, whether the citation is in a document (such as a case) or in a results list.

B. Sources of Citation Rules

There are many sources for citation rules. Nationally, two legal citation guides cover citation rules in great detail: *The Bluebook: A Uniform System of*

---

2. Remember that citations follow the practitioner form of the *Bluebook* and the *ALWD Guide* unless marked otherwise. While the 20th edition of the *Bluebook* allows practice documents to use large and small capitals as a font, that is not the custom and is not followed here.

3. *Black's Law Dictionary* 1335 (10th ed. 2014). For a more thorough discussion of how to avoid plagiarism, see Part XXVI(A) on Avoiding Plagiarism in Eugene Volokh, *Academic Legal Writing: Law Review Articles, Student Notes, Seminar Papers, and Getting on Law Review* (4th ed. 2010). Additional information is available on the website of the Legal Writing Institute at www.lwionline.org.

Table 12-2. Citation Information Important to Legal Researchers

Abbreviations	Meaning of Abbreviations to the Legal Researcher
U.S., S. Ct., and L. Ed.	A case decided in the United States Supreme Court.
F., F.2d, F.3d, and F. App'x	A case opinion from a federal court of appeals.
F., F.2d, and F.3d	A reported case opinion from a federal court of appeals.
F. Supp. and F. Supp. 2d	A reported case from a federal trial court.
A., N.E., N.W., P., S.E., S.W., and So. (including 2d and 3d series of each)	A case from a state court. (See Table T4-1 of this book for a list of the states whose cases are included in each of these regional reporters.)
Ohio St. (including 2d and 3d series)	A case from the Supreme Court of Ohio.
Ohio App. (including 2d and 3d series)	A reported case from an Ohio District Court of Appeals.
U.S.C., U.S.C.A, and U.S.C.S.	A federal statute.
Ohio Rev. Code, R.C., and O.R.C.	An Ohio statute.

Citation and the *ALWD Guide to Legal Citation*. The *Ohio Manual of Citations* governs the citation format used for Ohio state opinions. Additionally, the *Ohio Manual* is often used in court documents and by many attorneys. In law practice, you may encounter state statutes, court rules, and style manuals that dictate the form of citation used before the courts of different states. You may find that each firm or agency that you work for has its own citation system or makes minor variations to a generally accepted format. Some law offices have their own style manuals, drawn from state rules and national manuals. Once you are aware of the basic function and format of citation, adapting to a slightly different set of rules is not difficult.

C. Incorporating Citations into a Document

A legal document must provide a citation for each idea that comes from a case, statute, article, or other source. Thus, paragraphs that state legal rules and explain the law should contain many citations.

A citation may offer support for an entire sentence or for an idea expressed in part of a sentence. If the citation supports the entire sentence, it is placed in a separate *citation sentence* that begins with a capital letter and ends with a period. If the citation supports only a portion of the sentence, it is included immediately after the relevant part of that sentence and set off from the sentence by commas in what is called a *citation clause*. Table 12-3 provides examples of each.

Table 12-3. Examples of Citation Sentences and Citation Clauses

Citation Sentences: Voluntary manslaughter is knowingly causing the death of another while in a state of sudden passion or rage brought on by serious provocation of the victim. Ohio Rev. Code Ann. § 2903.03 (LexisNexis 2013). Words alone are not generally "reasonably sufficient provocation to incite the use of deadly force in most situations." *State v. Shane*, 590 N.E.2d 272, 278 (Ohio 1992). In each case, the trial judge must decide whether the facts, viewed in the light most favorable to the defendant, warrant the presentation of a voluntary manslaughter instruction to the jury. *Id.*

Citation Clauses: Ohio statutes define both voluntary manslaughter, *see* Ohio Rev. Code Ann. § 2903.03 (LexisNexis 2013), and involuntary manslaughter, *see* Ohio Rev. Code Ann. § 2903.04 (LexisNexis 2013).

D. Citations to Print and Online Versions

Generally, citations should be made to the format (i.e., print vs. online, official vs. commercial) of the source used. Traditionally, this format has been print sources, and current citation formats are structured for print materials. The *Ohio Manual* does not have different citation formats for sources available online or in print, and it is possible to compose complete and proper citations without resort to print materials. *Bluebook* Rule 18.2, however, explicitly requires the "use and citation of traditional printed sources when available, unless there is a digital copy of the source available that is authenticated, official, or an exact copy of the printed source, as described in rule 18.2.1." Rule 18 provides detailed instructions for how to cite to online sources, but these forms are not widely accepted either in practice or in academic publications such as law reviews. With print versions becoming increasingly unavailable and most legal researchers preferring to conduct research online, citing to online versions of sources may be necessary.

II. *Ohio Manual of Citations*[4]

The citation rules in the *Ohio Manual of Citations* govern the citation format used for Ohio state opinions. Additionally, these local rules are often used in court documents and by many Ohio attorneys. These rules are incorporated into the *Writing Manual: A Guide to Citations, Style and Judicial Opinion Writing* published and kept up-to-date by the Supreme Court of Ohio. The *Writing Manual* also includes a Style Guide, which covers some of the stylistic rules included in the *ALWD Guide* and the *Bluebook* such as capitalization, footnotes, italics, and quotations.

The *Ohio Manual of Citations* begins with rules for citing specific types of authority. Stylistic matters, such as italics, spacing, and capitalization, are found toward the end. Table 12-4 shows the structure of the *Ohio Manual of Citations*.

The current *Ohio Manual* is much more similar to the *Bluebook* and *ALWD Guide* than past editions. The most important differences are slight variations of abbreviations, including spacing.

Table 12-4. Structure of the *Ohio Manual of Citations*

Topics	Rules
General rules that apply to all types of citations, such as use of signals, typeface, abbreviations, short citation forms, etc.	Rule 6
Rules that apply to specific types of legal authority, such as cases, statutes, and regulations.	Rules 1–5

A. General Instructions for Citing Cases Under the *Ohio Manual of Citations*

The basic structure of a case citation contains the information needed to find the case in print. This structure is used even if the case is found and used online. The basic elements of a case citation are the party names, the reporter, volume, and page number, and a parenthetical including the court and year

---

4. Citations in this section conform to the requirements of the *Ohio Manual of Citations*.

of decision. Between the parties' names, place a lower case "v" followed by a period. Do not use a capital "V" or the abbreviation "vs."

The earlier example of the *Board of Education* case citation shows those three elements:

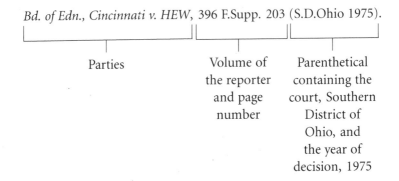

Bd. of Edn., Cincinnati v. HEW, 396 F.Supp. 203 (S.D.Ohio 1975).

Parties · Volume of the reporter and page number · Parenthetical containing the court, Southern District of Ohio, and the year of decision, 1975

1. Party Names

In legal memoranda and court documents, party names are italicized or underlined. For brevity, you will often need to abbreviate common words in a party name, such as "Board" and "Education." Rule 6.9 provides a list of common abbreviations used in case names as well as instructions for creating plurals of abbreviations.

2. Reporters

Abbreviations for Ohio and other reporters are incorporated into the rules for citing cases in Rule 1. For example, Rule 1.3, which deals with citing Ohio cases, includes a table of the abbreviations for reporters including Ohio cases.

Often, one case is published in multiple reporters, resulting in parallel citations. The following case is reported in four different publications: *Doyle v. Ohio*, 426 U.S. 610, 96 S.Ct. 2240, 54 U.S.L.W. 2230, 49 L.Ed. 2d 91 (1976). The *Ohio Manual* requires parallel citation of all cases when they are available.

3. Parentheticals

The citation as a whole should tell the reader which court decided the case and in what year. In some circumstances, the court is obvious from the reporter where the case is found, such as in *Doyle v. Ohio*, 426 U.S. 610 (1976). Since only U.S. Supreme Court opinions are published in *United States Reports* (U.S.), it is not necessary to specify the court in the parenthetical. However, the case in the earlier citation example, *Board of Education*, appears in the *Federal Sup-*

plement, which contains opinions of the many different federal district courts. In situations where the specific court is not clear from the reporter, include the court abbreviation in the parenthetical. The *Board of Education* case was decided by the U.S. District Court for the Southern District of Ohio, which is abbreviated S.D.Ohio.

4. Pinpoint Citations

Pinpoint citations direct the reader to a specific part of the opinion. A page or range of pages often follows the first page of the opinion:

Bd. of Edn., Cincinnati v. HEW, 396 F.Supp. 203, 205 (S.D.Ohio 1975).

Pinpoint
Citation

In this example, the citation refers the reader to page 205 of the opinion that begins at page 203. In Ohio cases decided after 2002, citations to specific paragraphs rather than pages are required, as shown below:

State v. Reed, 155 Ohio App.3d 435, 2003-Ohio-6536, 801 N.E.2d 862, ¶ 50–52.

This example has a pinpoint citation to paragraphs 50 through 52 in the opinion, rather than to the corresponding page number.

When using an online version of a case, remember that a reference to a specific reporter page may change in the middle of a computer screen or a printed page. This means that the page number indicated at the top of the screen or printed page may not be the page where the relevant information is located. For example, if the notation *206 appeared in the text before the relevant information, the pinpoint cite would be to page 206, not page 205.

5. Introductory Signals

Introductory signals characterize the type of support provided by the cited case. If the citing case directly supports the asserted proposition, then a signal is not used. However, in the following example, the signal *"see"* precedes the citation:

See Bd. of Edn., Cincinnati v. HEW, 396 F.Supp. 203 (S.D.Ohio 1975).

Signal

This signal indicates in shorthand that the cited case supports the asserted proposition implicitly. Table 12-5 contains a sample of signals and their respective meanings.

Table 12-5. Signals in the *Ohio Manual*

Signal	Meaning under *Ohio Manual*
No signal	Cited authority provides direct support. Use when quoting, paraphrasing, or explaining an authority.
See	Cited authority provides clear, but indirect support.
Accord	Additional authority provides direct support.
See also	Additional authority provides clear, but indirect support.
Compare	Used to compare an authority with another authority. ("Compare" is used instead of the *Bluebook*'s cf. signal.)
Contra	Cited authority directly states the contrary.
E.g.	Used instead of the disfavored string citation, *e.g.* indicates that the citing authority provides direct support and is representative of many authorities that are not cited.

The distinctions between these categories of support provided by a cited authority can be confusing. Remember that the absence of a signal indicates that the citing authority provides explicit, direct support for the proposition, while use of *see* signals implicit support. If you are unsure of what signal to use, consult Rule 6.2.

6. Prior and Subsequent History

Sometimes a case citation requires references to the case's prior or subsequent history. Inclusion of prior history, which consists of related case(s) decided before the case you are citing, is required only if that history is particularly relevant to an issue. Inclusion of subsequent history is generally required, with some exceptions. Consult Rule 6.4 for details. The earlier citation example includes a reference to its subsequent history:

See Bd. of Edn., Cincinnati v. HEW, 396 F. Supp. 203 (S.D.Ohio 1975), *aff'd in part and rev'd in part on other grounds*, 532 F.2d 1070 (C.A.6 1976).

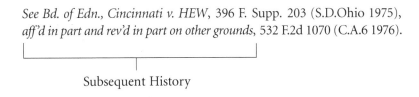

Subsequent History

B. Special Rules for Citing Particular Types of Ohio Cases

Remember that, in 2002, the Ohio Supreme Court drastically changed the way Ohio court opinions are published.[5] Before May 1, 2002, cases were either reported (i.e., appeared in print reporters) or unreported (i.e., did not appear in a print reporter). Reported cases were cited one way and unreported cases were cited in a different way. In 2002, the court did away with this distinction: all cases that appear on the court's website are now reported and are assigned a "WebCite." Thus, the first thing to determine before citing an Ohio case is whether it was decided before this date.

1. Citing Ohio Cases Decided Before May 1, 2002

a. Print Published (Reported) Cases

For Ohio cases decided before May 1, 2002, that appear in a print reporter, the citation contains three basic elements: the name of the case (properly abbreviated), information about all of the reporters in which the opinion appeared, and the court and year of the decision in parenthesis. Table 12-6 provides examples of reported Ohio cases decided before May 1, 2002.

Table 12-6. Example Ohio Reported Cases Decided Before May 1, 2002

Ohio Supreme Court	*Herrick v. Lindley*, 59 Ohio St.2d 22, 391 N.E.2d 729 (1979).
Ohio Court of Appeals	*State v. Brooks*, 133 Ohio App.3d 521, 728 N.E.2d 1119 (4th Dist. 1999).
Ohio Trial Court	*Guerra, Exr. v. Guerra*, 25 Ohio Misc. 1, 265 N.E.2d 818 (C.P.1970).

Notice in the *Ohio Manual of Citations* form that the parallel citation to the official reporter must be included along with the citation to the *North Eastern Reporter*. When the court is apparent from the parallel citations (e.g., only

---

5. For a thorough discussion of this change, see Chapter 4, Part II.A.

Supreme Court of Ohio decisions are published in *Ohio State Reports, 2d*), it is not necessary to designate the court in the parenthetical. Rule 1.1.B.3 includes the abbreviations for particular trial courts.

b. Cases Not Appearing in a Print Reporter

For cases that did not appear in a print reporter and were decided before May 1, 2002, the basic formula for citing cases includes the name of the case, the name of the specific court that decided the case, the case number preceded by "No.," an electronic database citation when available, and the month, day, and year of the decision. Table 12-7 provides examples of unreported Ohio cases decided before May 1, 2002.

Table 12-7. Example Ohio Unreported Cases Decided Before May 1, 2002

Ohio Court of Appeals	*Moton v. Ford Motor Credit Co.*, 5th Dist. Richland No. 01CA4, 2001 Ohio App. LEXIS 6094 (Dec. 17, 2001).
Ohio Trial Court	*State ex rel. Celebrezze v. Scandinavian Health Spa, Inc.*, Summit C.P. No. CV863-1158, 1986 WL 363150 (Mar. 31, 1986).

2. Citing Ohio Cases Decided After May 1, 2002

In 2002, the Supreme Court of Ohio began to make all Ohio appellate decisions, along with select trial court decisions, available on its website. Citations to Ohio opinions must include the reference to the court's web versions, called WebCite citations, when they are available. Here is an example of an Ohio WebCite citation:

2002-Ohio-7217

The first four numbers reflect the year of decision; they are followed by the state designation of Ohio, and the number unique to the specific case. Inclusion of the WebCite citation changes citation form quite a bit, as shown in the next example:

Ferrando v. Auto-Owners Ins. Co., 98 Ohio St.3d 186, 2002-Ohio-7217, 781 N.E.2d 927.

Note that the parenthetical containing the court and year of decision is completely omitted. That is because the WebCite citation (2002-Ohio-7217) includes the year of decision and the official reporter citation (98 Ohio St.3d 186) indicates that this is a decision of the Supreme Court of Ohio. Hence, it is not necessary to add those two pieces of information in a parenthetical.

Some cases decided before 2002 have been given a WebCite. If they have numbered paragraphs, as described in the next section, they should also be cited this way.

Another post-May 2002 difference in citation form is found in the expression of pinpoint citations. Each paragraph in the text of an Ohio opinion published on the Supreme Court of Ohio's website is now assigned a paragraph number. Table 12-8 contains an excerpt from a recent Supreme Court of Ohio opinion that uses paragraph numbers.

Table 12-8. Excerpt from an Ohio Supreme Court Opinion

CLEVELAND BAR ASSOCIATION V. JAMES. 109 Ohio St.3d 310, 2006-Ohio-2424.

Per Curiam.

{¶ **1**} Respondent, Ronald Dennis James of Shaker Heights, Ohio, Attorney Registration No. 0041120, was admitted to the Ohio bar in 1977.

{¶ **2**} On February 7, 2005, relator, Cleveland Bar Association, filed a complaint charging respondent with professional misconduct. Attempts to serve respondent by certified mail were unsuccessful, and the complaint was served on the Clerk of the Supreme Court pursuant to Gov.Bar R. V(11)(B).

....

{¶ **8**} We agree with relator that respondent should be suspended from the practice of law for one year. Attorneys must timely respond to a disciplinary inquiry, whether the inquiry relates to the lawyer's own conduct or that of a colleague. Compliance with this obligation is critical to the effectiveness of the legal profession's effort to monitor itself. Although every communication from a disciplinary agency should be taken seriously, the initial inquiry about a client ...

Source: *Ohio Official Reports*. Reprinted with permission of the Supreme Court of Ohio's Reporter of Decision.

Note that each paragraph is numbered (i.e., ¶ 8). So for pinpoint citations, rather than citing a specific page number, attorneys cite the specific paragraph number(s), as shown below:

State v. Reed, 155 Ohio App.3d 435, 2003-Ohio-6536, 801 N.E.2d 862, ¶ 50–52.

This example has a pinpoint citation to paragraphs 50 through 52 in the opinion, rather than to the corresponding page number.

a. Print Published Cases

For cases decided after May 1, 2002, that appear in a print reporter, the basic formula is the full name of the case (properly abbreviated), information about all of the reporters in which the opinion appeared, the WebCite, and any information about the court, jurisdiction, or year that isn't apparent from the rest of the citation. The official print reporters for Ohio appellate and trial cases ceased publication in 2012. Therefore, it is possible that cases decided in 2012 and later have only a WebCite and a *North Eastern Reporter* citation. Table 12-9 provides examples of print published Ohio cases decided after May 1, 2002.

Table 12-9. Example Ohio Print Published Cases Decided After May 1, 2002

Ohio Supreme Court	*Snyder v. Ohio Dept. of Natural Resources*, 140 Ohio St.3d 322, 2014-Ohio-3942, 18 N.E.3d 416.
Ohio Court of Appeal (officially print published)	*Friedland v. Djukic*, 191 Ohio App.3d 278, 2010-Ohio-5777, 945 N.E.2d 1095.
Ohio Court of Appeal (print published, no official print publication)	*In re W.C.*, 2013-Ohio-153, 986 N.E.2d 572 (12th Dist.).
Ohio Trial Court (officially print published)	*Himmelsbach-Preston v. Royal Custom Cleaners*, 136 Ohio Misc.2d 34, 2005-Ohio-7145, 847 N.E.2d 75 (M.C.).

b. Non-Print Published Cases

Remember that all cases from the Ohio Supreme Court are published both in a print reporter and on the court's website. For appellate and trial court cases that are not published in a print reporter, the *Ohio Manual* requires that the citation include the name of the case, and both the appellate district and the county of the case, the WebCite (when it is available), and an electronic database citation (e.g., a Westlaw or Lexis citation) when the WebCite is not available. Thus, the citation format for Ohio cases not published in a standard print reporter (meaning the case is "non-print published" as described in Chapter 4) depends upon whether there is a WebCite citation available. For cases for which there is no WebCite available, use the citation format for similar cases decided prior to May 1, 2002. Table 12-10 provides examples of non-print published cases decided after May 1, 2002.

**Table 12-10. Example Ohio Non-print Published Cases
Decided On or After May 1, 2002**

Ohio Court of Appeal (WebCite not available)	*State v. Sampson*, 1st Dist. Hamilton No. C-10547, 2002 Ohio App. LEXIS 2020 (May 1, 2002).
Ohio Court of Appeal (WebCite available)	*Brooks v. All America*, 3d Dist. Shelby No. 17-02-25, 2002-Ohio-6617.
Ohio Trial Court (WebCite available)	*Flores v. Bowling Green State Univ.*, Ct. of Cl. No. 2012-07153, 2013-Ohio-4864.
Ohio Trial Court (WebCite not available)	*Brown v. Taji*, Lucas C.P. No. CI99-2697, 2004 WL 3799447 (Mar. 1, 2004).

C. Citing Cases from Other State Jurisdictions

In citing cases from other states, the *Ohio Manual of Citations* requires citation to both the official reporter and parallel citations, where available. Here is an example of a citation where the opinion appears in an official reporter:

Richards v. Anderson, 9 Utah 2d 17, 337 P.2d 59 (1959).

Note the parenthetical, placed after the party names, only contains the year. That is because the court is apparent from the reporter abbreviation: "Utah 2d." Looking up Utah in Table T1 of the *Bluebook* or in Appendix 1 of the *ALWD Guide* shows that only Utah Supreme Court decisions appear in this reporter.

Many states have chosen not to publish their own official court reports and instead rely on the West regional reporters for publication of their opinions. If an official reporter is not available and the case only appears in a West regional reporter (such as *North Eastern Reporter*), then it is necessary to specify the court in the parenthetical. The following example shows a citation to an opinion that appears only in the regional reporter:

Lawley v. Kansas City, 516 S.W.2d 829 (Mo.App.1974).

Since the *South Western Reporter, 2d Series* (S.W.2d) contains opinions of numerous states and decisions of the highest as well as intermediate appellate courts, it is necessary to specify the state and court level in the parenthetical. The *Ohio Manual of Citations* lists abbreviations for other state reports and the West regional reporters on pages 29–36.

D. Citing Cases from Federal Courts

As with other types of cases, for cases from federal courts, the *Ohio Manual of Citations* requires citation to both the official reporter and parallel citations when available. Table 12-11 provides examples of citations to federal cases.

Table 12-11. Example Federal Case Citations

United States Supreme Court	*Meritor Savs. Bank v. Vinson*, 477 U.S. 57, 106 S.Ct. 2399, 91 L.Ed.2d 49 (1986).
Federal Court of Appeal	*Allabani v. Gonzales*, 402 F.3d 668 (6th Cir. 2005).
Federal District Court	*Mosley v. Bowen*, 703 F.Supp. 1288 (S.D.Ohio 1989).

E. Citing Statutes and Regulations

The *Ohio Manual of Citations* requires citation to statutes and regulations as they appear in the statutory code or compilation. The citation typically contains an abbreviation for the code as well as the numerical designation for the section.

There are two main differences between federal and Ohio code citations. First, although there is one official version of the United States Code, in Ohio there is no official version of the Ohio Revised Code. Second, although the citations to federal and Ohio statutes and regulations contain the same pieces of information, those pieces are arranged differently in the respective federal and Ohio citations. Since section numbers in the Ohio Revised Code and the Ohio Administrative Code include the corresponding title number, it is not necessary to list the title number separately. Rules 3 and 4 provide the appropriate abbreviations for the codes. Note that no abbreviations are used when referring to municipal codes (often called ordinances). Table 12-12 provides examples of how to cite to state and federal statutes.

Table 12-12. Example Code Citations

Ohio Revised Code	R.C. 2903.03.
United States Code	7 U.S.C. 6503.
Out of State Statutes	Tex.Penal Code 3.02.
Ohio Administrative Code	Ohio Adm.Code 3307-1-03.
Code of Federal Regulations	7 C.F.R. 205.1.
Ohio Municipal Ordinance	Lima Codified Ordinances 476.01.

When citing to historical versions of code sections, refer to Rules 3 and 4 of the *Ohio Manual* for the detailed requirements.

F. Secondary Sources

A few commonly cited secondary sources are specifically mentioned in the *Ohio Manual of Citations*. The format for commonly cited texts, treatises, and dictionaries can be found on page 51 of the *Ohio Manual*. Additionally, the *Ohio Manual* has specific rules for legal encyclopedias (Rule 5.5), law reviews (Rule 5.3), and Restatements (Rule 5.1). Table 12-13 compares citations to legal encyclopedia, Restatements, and law review articles.

Table 12-13. Citations to Secondary Sources

	Ohio Manual of Citations
Legal encyclopedia	16 Ohio Jurisprudence 3d, Condominiums and Co-operative Apartments, Section 20 (2010).
Law review article	John Quigley, *Ohio's Unique Rule on Burden of Persuasion for Self-Defense: Unraveling the Legislative and Judicial Tangle,* 20 U.Tol.L.Rev. 105 (1988).
Restatement	1 Restatement of the Law 2d, Contracts, Section 159 (1981).

G. Short-Form Citations

Short-form citations are used after the first time you cite a source. The *Ohio Manual* has no strict rules for composing short-form citations. Generally for cases, including the first named party and a page or paragraph number for a case short-form citation is acceptable. Examples of acceptable short-form citations are included on pages 59–62.

III. The *Bluebook and ALWD Guide*

As noted earlier, there are two national citation manuals. Student editors of four Ivy League law reviews have developed citation rules that are published as *The Bluebook: A Uniform System of Citation*, now in its 20th edition. For most of the last century, the *Bluebook* was the only national citation system that was widely recognized. Rather than an easy-to-understand guide that you can read cover-to-cover to understand legal citation, the *Bluebook* is somewhat difficult to grasp at first.

Although law firms, agencies, and organizations consider *Bluebook* citations the norm, many practicing lawyers do not know its current rules; most assume that the *Bluebook* rules have not changed since they were in law school.

Begun in 2000 by the Association of Legal Writing Directors, the *ALWD Guide* seeks to provide a user-friendly guide to the standard legal citation rules developed in the *Bluebook* and other citation systems. The current *ALWD Guide* is designed to produce citations that are identical to those created with the *Bluebook*.

The key to mastering the *Bluebook* and the *ALWD Guide* is to first understand their respective structures, which are quite similar. Table 12-14 outlines this structure. The rest of this part of the chapter explains citations with the *Bluebook* and the *ALWD Guide*. Sections A through H below explain how to use the current *Bluebook* and *ALWD* rules in writing memoranda and briefs, along with fundamental citation rules. Section I explains how to use the current *Bluebook* and *ALWD* rules in writing articles for scholarly publication.

Table 12-14. Structure of the *Bluebook* and the *ALWD Guide*

Rules	Bluebook	ALWD Guide
General rules that apply to all types of citations, such as use of signals, typeface, abbreviations, short citation forms, etc.	B1–B9, Rules 1–9	Rules 1–11 and 34–40
Rules that apply to specific types of legal authority, such as cases, statutes, and regulations.	B10–B21 Rules 10–21	Rules 12–33
Abbreviations and citation format for primary sources in each jurisdiction (i.e., federal, all fifty states, etc.).	Table T1 (U.S. Federal and State) Table T2 (Foreign Jurisdictions) Table T3 (International Organizations)	Appendix 1 (U.S. Federal, State, Territories and Tribal sources) Appendix 6 (U.S. Federal Tax) Appendix 7 (U.S. Federal agency documents)
Abbreviations for case names, court names, months, etc.	Tables T6–T16	Appendices 3–5

A. Citations for Practice Documents

The two national citation manuals include *two* citation systems: one for law review articles and another for legal memoranda and court documents. Most of the *Bluebook*'s over 500 pages are devoted to citations used for articles published in law journals. The rules most important to attorneys, those concerning legal memoranda and court documents, are given less attention in the *Bluebook* but are covered first below. Remember that the examples in the body of the *Bluebook* are in law review style. When writing a document other than a law review article, you will need to refer also to the Bluepages at the front of the book and the examples inside the back cover to see how you must modify the examples. The *ALWD Guide*, in contrast, focuses on citations for practice documents and marks examples specifically formatted for law reviews with an "Academic Formatting" icon.

1. *Bluebook* Quick Reference Guides

Perhaps the most helpful information in the *Bluebook* is the reference guide on the inside back cover of the book, which gives examples of citations used in court documents and legal memoranda.[6] Another helpful portion of the *Bluebook* appears on pages 3 through 56; these are the "Bluepages," which were introduced in the 18th edition. Previous editions contained a much shorter section called "Practitioner's Notes."

Bluepages provide information for and additional examples of citations used in documents other than law review articles. Bluepages Rule B2 covers typeface and explains that typically only italics, underlining, and ordinary roman type should be used in citations in legal memoranda and court documents. B2 then lists those items that should be italicized or underlined, including case names, titles of books and articles, and introductory signals. Items not included in the list should appear in regular type.

2. Index

The indices at the back of both the *Bluebook* and *ALWD Guide* are quite extensive, and in most instances it is more helpful than the table of contents. Most often, you should begin working by referring to the index.

---

6. Examples of law review citations are found on the inside front cover of the *Bluebook*.

B. Cases

Because Ohio has adopted a Public Domain Format (the WebCite), the *Bluebook* requires that the jurisdiction's form should be observed. So, for cases decided after May 1, 2002, with a WebCite, the *Ohio Manual of Citations* form should be used. *Bluebook* Rule 10.3.3; *ALWD* Rule 12.17.

Cases decided before May 1, 2002, or cases without a WebCite can still be cited according to *Bluebook* or *ALWD* form. This form is explained in detail below, although the essentials are very similar to the Ohio citations discussed earlier in this chapter. A full citation to a case includes (1) the name of the case, (2) the volume and reporter in which the case is published, (3) the first page of the case, (4) the exact page in the case that contains the idea you are citing (i.e., the *pinpoint* or *jump cite*), (5) the court that decided the case, and (6) the date the case was decided. The key points for citation to cases are given below, along with examples. *Bluebook* Rule 10 and *ALWD* Rule 12 cover case citations in detail.

1. Essential Components of Case Citations

Include the name of just the first party on each side, even if several are listed in the case caption. If the party is an individual, include only the party's last name. If the party is a business or organization, shorten the party's name by using the abbreviations in *Bluebook* Table T6 or *ALWD* Appendix 3.

The parties' names may be italicized or underlined. Use the style preferred by your supervisor, and use that style consistently throughout each document. Do not combine italics and underlining in one cite or within a single document.

Place a comma after the second party's name; do not italicize or underline this comma.

> EXAMPLE: *Harris v. Fla. Elections Comm'n*, 235 F.3d 578, 580
> (11th Cir. 2000).

Next, give the volume and the reporter in which the case is found. Pay special attention to whether the reporter is in its first, second, or third series. Abbreviations for reporters are found in *Bluebook* Table T1 and *ALWD* Appendix 1. In the example above, 235 is the volume number and F.3d is the reporter abbreviation for *Federal Reporter, Third Series.*

After the reporter name, include both the first page of the case and the pinpoint page containing the idea that you are referencing, separated by a comma and a space. The first page of the *Harris* case above is 578, and the page containing the specific idea being cited is 580. If the pinpoint page you are citing is also the first page of the case, then the same page number will appear twice even though this is repetitive.

In a parenthetical following this information, indicate the court that decided the case, using abbreviations in *Bluebook* Table T1 or *ALWD* Appendices 1, 3, and 4. In the above example, the United States Court of Appeals for the Eleventh Circuit, a federal court, decided the case.

If the reporter abbreviation clearly indicates which court decided a case, do not repeat this information in the parenthetical. To give two examples, only cases of the United States Supreme Court are reported in *United States Reports*, abbreviated U.S. Only cases decided by the Supreme Court of Ohio are reported in *Ohio State Reports*, which is abbreviated Ohio St. Repeating court abbreviations in citations to those reporters would be duplicative. By contrast, *North Eastern Reporter, 2d*, abbreviated N.E.2d, publishes decisions from different courts within several states, so the court that decided a particular case needs to be indicated parenthetically. Thus, in the last example below in Table 12-15, "Ohio Ct. App." indicates that the decision came from the Ohio Court of Appeals rather than from another court whose decisions are also published in this reporter.

Table 12-15. Examples of Reported Cases in *Bluebook/ALWD* Citation

Ohio Supreme Court Case	*Herrick v. Lindley*, 391 N.E.2d 729 (Ohio 1979).
Ohio Court of Appeals Case	*State v. Brooks*, 728 N.E.2d 1119 (Ohio Ct. App. 1999).
United States Supreme Court Case	*Citizens United v. Fed. Election Comm'n*, 558 U.S. 310, 323 (2010).

The final piece of required information in most cites is the date the case was decided. For cases published in reporters, give only the year of decision, not the month or date. Do not confuse the date of decision with the date on which the case was argued or submitted, the date on which a motion for rehearing was denied, or the publication date of the reporter. For cases that are unreported, give the month abbreviation, date, and year.

2. Full and Short Citations to Cases

The first time you mention a case by name, immediately give its full citation, including all of the information outlined above. Even though it is technically correct to include the full citation at the beginning of a sentence, a full citation takes up considerable space. By the time a reader gets through the citation and to your idea at the end of the sentence, the reader may have lost interest. The examples in Table 12-16 demonstrate this problem.

Table 12-16. Examples of Full Citations

Assume that this is the first time the case has been mentioned in this document. Both versions are correct, but the second should be avoided.

The law assumes that jurors in a trial will follow the judge's instructions. *State v. Thompson*, 141 Ohio St.3d 254, 2014-Ohio-4751, 23 N.E.3d 1096, ¶ 150.

In *State v. Thompson*, 141 Ohio St.3d 254, 2014-Ohio-4751, 23 N.E.3d 1096, ¶ 150, the court noted that it assumed that the jury followed the judge's instructions.

After a full citation has been used once to introduce an authority, short citations are subsequently used to cite to this same authority. A short citation provides just enough information to allow the reader to locate the longer citation and find the pinpoint page.

When the immediately preceding citation is to the same source and the same page or paragraph number, use *id.* as the short cite. When the second cite is to a different page or paragraph number within the same source, follow the *id.* with "at" and the new pinpoint page or paragraph number. Capitalize *id.* when it begins a citation sentence, but not when it follows a signal or appears in a citation clause.

If the citation is from a case that is not the immediately preceding citation, give the name of one of the parties (generally the first party named in the full cite), the volume, the reporter, and the pinpoint page following "at."

EXAMPLE: A showing of adverse possession requires that a claimant demonstrate exclusive possession and open, notorious, continuous, and adverse use of land for twenty-one years. *Grace v. Koch*, 692 N.E.2d 1009, 1010 (Ohio 1998). Failure to prove any single element defeats the claim of adverse possession. *Id.* The claimant bears the burden of proving adverse possession by clear and convincing evidence. *Id.* at 1012. The subjective intent of a claimant is not relevant; it is the nature of the possession which must be adverse. *Evanich v. Bridge*, 119 Ohio St. 3d 260, 2008-Ohio-3820, 893 N.E.2d 481, ¶ 8–10. Seeking permission before entering the land of another negates any adverse intent. *Grace*, 692 N.E.2d at 1013.

If you refer to the case by name in the sentence, your short citation does not need to repeat the case name, though lawyers often do. The last sentence of the example would also be correct as follows: "In *Grace*, the court found that seeking permission before entering the land of another negates any adverse intent. 692 N.E.2d at 1013."

The format, *Grace* at 1013, consisting of just a case name and page number, is incorrect. The volume and reporter abbreviation are also needed.

3. Prior and Subsequent History

Sometimes a citation needs to show what happened to a case at an earlier or later stage of litigation. The case you are citing may have reversed an earlier case, as in the example below. If you are citing a case for a court's analysis of one issue and a later court reversed only on the second issue, you need to alert your reader to that reversal. Or, if you decide for historical purposes to include in a document discussion of a case that was later overruled, your reader needs to know that as soon as you introduce the case. Prior and subsequent history can be appended to the full citations discussed above.

> EXAMPLE: The only time that the Supreme Court addressed the require-
> ment of motive for an EMTALA claim, the Court rejected that
> requirement. *Roberts v. Galen of Va.*, 525 U.S. 249, 253 (1999),
> *rev'g* 111 F.3d 405 (6th Cir. 1997).

C. Codes

Generally a statute or regulation is cited as it appears in the code or compilation. The citation typically contains the following information: the title number of the code, the abbreviation for the compilation or code, the specific section(s) being referenced, the publisher (if using a commercially published code), and the year the statutory code was published or, if using an online resource, its currency. Note that the date given in statutory and regulation citations is the date of the print volume in which the statute is published, not the date the statute was enacted or the regulation was promulgated. Table 12-17 contains examples of citations to statutory and regulatory codes.

Table 12-17. Examples of Statutory and Regulatory Code Citations

U.S. Code (current statutory language appears in the official print code)	12 U.S.C. § 222 (2012).
U.S. Code (current statutory language is too new to appear in the official code and appears in both the bound volume and the supplement)	33 U.S.C.A. § 1321 (West 2001 & Supp. 2014).
U.S. Code (current statutory language is too new to appear in the official code and appears in just the supplement)	22 U.S.C.A. § 8803 (West Supp. 2014).
U.S. Code (citing to the online version)	26 U.S.C.A. § 1400 (Westlaw current through P.L. 113-296).
Page's Ohio Revised Code Annotated in print	Ohio Rev. Code Ann. § 5711.34 (Lexis-Nexis 2013).
Baldwin's Ohio Revised Code Annotated online	Ohio Rev. Code Ann. § 1509.35 (Westlaw current through 2015 Files 1, 3 and 4 of the 131st GA (2015–16)).
Ohio Administrative Code	Ohio Admin. Code 109:4-3-09 (2012).
Code of Federal Regulations	29 C.F.R. § 101.18(a) (2014).

The general rule for citing federal laws, set out in *Bluebook* Rule 12 and *ALWD* Rule 14, is to cite the *United States Code* (U.S.C.), which is the official code for federal statutes. In reality, that publication is published so slowly that the current language may be found in a commercial code, either *United States Code Annotated* (published by West) or *United States Code Service* (published by LexisNexis). If the language of a portion of the statute is reprinted in the pocket part, include the dates of both the bound volume and the pocket part. If the language appears only in the pocket part, include only the date of the pocket part.

Consult Table T1 of the *Bluebook* and Appendix 1 of the *ALWD Guide* for the proper statutory compilation abbreviations and citation order for all statutes, including Ohio.

Federal and state regulations are covered in Rule 14 of the Bluebook and Rule 18 of the *ALWD Guide.*

D. Constitutions

Citations to constitutions include the name of the constitution and the relevant article, part, clause, or amendment information. Unless you are citing to a repealed or outdated provision, no date information is necessary. Table 12-18 contains examples of citations to both the federal and Ohio constitutions in the *Bluebook/ALWD* format.

Table 12-18. Examples of Constitutional Citations

Federal constitution	U.S. Const. art. II, § 2, cl. 3.
Ohio constitution	Ohio Const. art. I, § 19.

E. Secondary Sources

Secondary sources are covered in detail in the *Bluebook* and the *ALWD Guide*. Consult the appropriate rules before writing a citation. Table 12-19 contains citations to the same secondary sources included in Table 12-13, simply for purposes of comparing the *Ohio Manual* formal to the *Bluebook/ALWD* form.

Table 12-19. Secondary Source Citations in *Bluebook/ALWD* Form

Legal Encyclopedia	16 Ohio Jur. 3d *Condominiums & Co-operative Apartments* § 20 (2010).
Law Review Article	John Quigley, *Ohio's Unique Rule on Burden of Persuasion for Self-Defense: Unraveling the Legislative and Judicial Tangle*, 20 U. Tol. L. Rev. 105 (1988).
Restatement	Restatement (Second) of Contracts § 159 (1981).

F. Signals

A citation must show the level of support each authority provides. You do this by deciding whether to use an introductory signal and, if so, which one. The more common signals are explained in Table 12-20.

Table 12-20. Common *Bluebook/ALWD* Signals

Signal	Definition
No Signal	The source directly states the idea in the sentence. The cite identifies the source of a quotation
See	The source cited offers implicit support for the idea in the sentence.
See also	The source cited provides additional support for the idea in the sentence. The support offered by the *see also* may not as strong or direct as authorities preceded by no signal or the signal *see*.
E.g.	Many authorities state the idea in the sentence, and you are citing only one as an example; this signal allows you to cite just one source while letting the reader know that many other sources say the same thing.

G. Quotations

Quotations should be used only when the reader needs to see the text exactly as it appears in the original authority. Of all legal audiences, trial courts are probably most receptive to longer quotations. For example, quoting the controlling statutory language can be extremely helpful. As another example, if a well-known case explains an analytical point in a particularly insightful way, a quotation may be warranted.

Excessive quotation has two drawbacks. First, quotations interrupt the flow of your writing when the style of the quoted language differs from your own. Second, excessive use of quotations may suggest to the reader that you do not fully comprehend the material; it is much easier to cut and paste together a document from pieces of various cases than to synthesize and explain a rule of law. Quotations should not be used simply because you cannot think of another way to express an idea.

When a quotation is needed, the words, punctuation, and capitalization within the quotation marks must appear *exactly* as they are in the original. Treat a quotation as a photocopy of the original text. Any alterations or omissions must be indicated. Include commas and periods inside quotation marks;

place other punctuation outside the quotation marks unless it is included in the original text. Also, try to provide smooth transitions between your text and the quoted text. If a quotation is more than 50 words, it must appear in a block quote (indenting the text on both the right and left sides). Consult *Bluebook* Rule 5 and *ALWD* Rule 38 for more information.

H. Citation Details

The following citation details deserve special note because they frequently trip up novices.

- Use proper ordinal abbreviations. The most confusing are 2d for "Second" and 3d for "Third" because they differ from the standard format. For an example of this use of ordinal numbers, see *Bluebook* Rule 6.2(b) or *ALWD* Rule 4.3.

- Do not insert a space between abbreviations of single capital letters. For example, there is no space in U.S. Ordinal numbers like 1st, 2d, and 3d are considered single capital letters for purposes of this rule. Thus, there is no space in S.E.2d or F.3d because 2d and 3d are considered single capital letters. Leave one space between elements of an abbreviation that are not single capital letters. For example, F. Supp. 2d has a space on each side of "Supp." It would be incorrect to write F.Supp.2d. For general rules on spacing, consult *Bluebook* Rule 6 or *ALWD* Rule 2.2.

- In citation sentences, abbreviate case names, court names, months, and reporter names. Do not abbreviate these words when they are part of textual sentences unless the abbreviations are "widely known"; instead, spell them out as in the example below. *Bluebook* Rules 10.2.1(c) and 10.2.2; *ALWD* Rule 2.

  EXAMPLE: The Ninth Circuit held that Oregon's Measure 11 did not violate constitutional rights provided under the Eighth and Fourteenth Amendments. *Alvarado v. Hill,* 252 F.3d 1066, 1069–70 (9th Cir. 2001).

- When *id.* is used to show support for just part of a sentence, this short cite is set off from the sentence by commas and is not capitalized. *See Bluebook* Rule 1.1; *ALWD* Rule 34.1(b).

- It is most common in legal documents to spell out numbers zero through ninety-nine and to use numerals for larger numbers. However, always spell out a number that is the first word of a sentence. *Bluebook* Rule 6.2(a); *ALWD* Rule 4.

I. Citations for Law Review Articles

Under both the *Bluebook* and the *ALWD Guide*, the citations for law review footnotes are different from those for practice documents. However, the two manuals produce the identical citations. Table 12-21 of this chapter summarizes the typeface used for several common sources and gives examples.

Table 12-21. *Bluebook/ALWD* Typeface for Law Review Footnotes

Item	Type Used	Example
Cases	Use ordinary type for case names in full citations.	Legal Servs. Corp. v. Velazquez, 531 U.S. 533 (2001).
Books	Use large and small capital letters for the author and the title.	MEGAN MCALPIN, BEYOND THE FIRST DRAFT (2014).
Periodical articles	Use ordinary type for the author's name, italics for the title, and large and small capitals for the periodical.	Adell Louise Amos, *The Use of State Instream Flow Laws for Federal Land: Respecting State Control While Meeting Federal Purposes*, 36 ENVIR. LAW 1237 (2006).
Explanatory phrases	Use italics for all explanatory phrases such as *aff'g*, *cert. denied*, *rev'd*, and *overruled by*.	Legal Servs. Corp. v. Velazquez, 531 U.S. 533 (2001), *aff'g* 164 F.3d 757 (2d Cir. 1999).
Introductory signals	Use italics for all introductory signals, such as *see* and *e.g.* when they appear in citations, as opposed to text.	*See id.*

Law review articles place citations in footnotes or endnotes, instead of placing citations in the main text of the document. Most law review footnotes include text in ordinary type, in italics, and in large and small capital letters. This convention is not universal, and each law review selects the typefaces it will use. Some law reviews may use only ordinary type and italics. Others may use just ordinary type.

The typeface used for a case name depends on (1) whether the case appears in the main text of the article or in a footnote and (2) how the case is used.

When a case name appears in the main text of the article or in a textual sentence of a footnote, it is italicized. By contrast, if a footnote contains an embedded citation, the case name is written in ordinary Roman type. Similarly, when a full cite is given in a footnote, the case name is written in ordinary type. But when a short cite is used in footnotes, the case name is italicized. Assuming you are submitting an article to a law review that uses all three typefaces, *Bluebook* Rule 2 and *ALWD* Rule 1.4 and Chart 1.3 dictate which typeface to use for each type of authority.

Short cites in law review footnotes are similar to short cites in other documents. The short cite *id.* can be used only if the preceding footnote contains only one authority. One unique *Bluebook* requirement is the "rule of five." This rule states that a short form citation, including "*id*" can be used if the source is "*readily found in one of the preceding five footnotes.*" *Bluebook* Rule 10.9.

IV. Editing Citations

To be sure that the citations in a document correctly reflect your research and support your analysis, include enough time in the writing and editing process to check citation accuracy. While writing the document, refer frequently to the local rules or to the citation guide required by your supervisor. After you have completely finished writing the text of the document, check the citations carefully again. Be sure that each citation is still accurate after all the writing revisions you have made. For example, moving a sentence might require you to change an *id.* to another form of short cite, or vice versa. In fact, some careful writers do not insert *id.* citations until they are completely finished writing and revising.

Sometimes editing for citations can take as long as editing for writing mechanics. The time invested in citations is well spent if it enables the person reading your document to quickly find the authorities you cite and to understand your analysis.

V. Deciphering Legal Abbreviations

At some point, you will likely encounter a citation containing a legal abbreviation that is difficult to translate. Numerous resources are available to help decipher unfamiliar legal abbreviations. A good place to start is the online Cardiff's Index to Legal Abbreviations.[7] Once there, you can search its database

---

7. This resource is freely available at www.legalabbrevs.cardiff.ac.uk.

by abbreviation and get a list of corresponding legal sources. If this fails to translate the abbreviation, two other sources might be helpful: *Prince's Bieber Dictionary of Legal Abbreviations* (6th ed. 2009), which is also available on Lexis, and the *Ohio Legal Research Guide* (1997), which contains a comprehensive table of Ohio abbreviations.

Appendix A

Ohio Research Guides

I. Online Ohio Research Guides

Cleveland–Marshall College of Law (CSU), Ohio Primary Law Legal Research Guide

http://guides.law.csuohio.edu/ohio_primary_law

> This comprehensive guide to Ohio legal research covers legislation, legislative history, constitutional history and research, administrative law, and case law.

Cleveland–Marshall College of Law (CSU), Ohio Secondary Sources Research Guide

http://guides.law.csuohio.edu/ohio_secondary

> This guide offers an overview and links to Ohio secondary sources such as encyclopedias, practice books, form books and databases, jury instructions, blogs, and news sources.

Ohio Legislative Service Commission, Members Only Briefs

www.lsc.state.oh.us/membersonly

> The Ohio Legislative Service Commission publishes a series of research reports on various legal topics for use by the Ohio General Assembly. *A Guide to Legislative History in Ohio* provides a good explanation of the numerous types of legislative history documents in Ohio.

Supreme Court of Ohio, Law Library Information Series

www.supremecourtofohio.gov/publications/lib_series/default.asp

> The Supreme Court of Ohio publishes a variety of pamphlets, many of which cover legal research topics.

CALI Ohio Legal Materials: Primary Sources
http://www.cali.org/lesson/1264

> Available to students at CALI member schools, this tutorial provides an interactive overview of Ohio cases, statutes, administrative materials, and court rules.

CALI Ohio Secondary Sources
http://www.cali.org/lesson/8999

> Available to students at CALI member schools, this tutorial provides an interactive overview of Ohio encyclopedias, practice books, form books, continuing legal education materials, law reviews, and news sources.

University of Cincinnati College of Law, Research Resources
http://guides.libraries.uc.edu/lawlibrary

> The University of Cincinnati College of Law Library offers numerous research guides, including several dedicated to Ohio.

University of Akron School of Law Library
http://law.uakron.libguides.com/ohiolaw

> This guide provides an overview of Ohio cases, statutes, regulations, and legislative history. It also includes resources for those who choose to represent themselves in Ohio courts.

Zimmerman's Research Guides on Ohio
www.lexisnexis.com/infopro/zimmermans/

> The list of Ohio research guides (accessible by browsing under "O") includes the following entries:
>
> • Executive Branch — Administrative Code and Regulations
> • Executive Branch — Agencies and Offices
> • Judicial Branch
> • Legislative Branch
> • Other Useful Information

II. Print Research Guides

Melanie K. Putnam & Susan M. Schaefgen, *Ohio Legal Research Guide* (1997).

Written as a reference resource, this book provides detailed information on the availability of most Ohio legal research sources. Although out of date, it is still the best source for older Ohio materials.

Kenneth S. Kozlowski & Susan N. Elliot, *Ohio Practice Materials: A Selective Annotated Bibliography*, in *State Practice Materials: Annotated Bibliographies* (Frank G. Houdek ed., 2002).

Also a reference resource, this bibliography lists by subject the current legal publications available. There are also chapters on other states included in the book as well. This book is available in the Spinelli's Law Library Reference Shelf on HeinOnline.

Steven H. Steinglass & Gino J. Scarselli, *The Ohio State Constitution* (2011).

A useful source if researching an Ohio Constitutional issue. The introduction offers an overview of the history of the Ohio Constitution followed by a section-by-section analysis of the current Constitution.

Appendix B

Important Legal Research Terminology and Abbreviations

Advance sheets	Soft-bound supplements to reporters.
Annotations	Generally, notes and commentary that include citations to other relevant authority.
BCite	Specifically, using Bloomberg Law's BCite tool rather than KeyCite or Shepard's for this research.
Case	A document written by a court to explain its decision in a particular dispute; also called a judicial opinion.
Citator	A research tool that provides a list of legal sources that have cited a particular case, statute, or other document.
Code	A subject arrangement of statutes, regulations, or municipal ordinances.
Compiled legislative history	A complete set of documents generated as a bill becomes a law.
Digest	An index to case law.
Docket number	A unique number assigned by the clerk of courts to each case.
Enabling statute	The legislation that gives an agency the authority to promulgate regulations.
G.C.	General Code (Ohio's second codification of statutes; in effect from 1910 to 1952).
GA	Ohio General Assembly.

General Assembly	The formal name of the Ohio legislature. It is bicameral (i.e., composed of a House and a Senate).
Headnote	A sentence or short paragraph, typically written by a publisher's staff, that sets out a single point of law in a case.
History note	The information added usually after the text of a statute (or regulation) that indicates when it was first enacted (or promulgated) and lists references where subsequent amendments can be found.
Index	A list of narrow topics covered by a source, usually found at the end of a work.
JCARR	Joint Committee on Agency Rule Review; the legislative committee charged with reviewing Ohio regulations.
Judicial opinion	A document written by a court to explain its decision in a particular dispute; also called a case.
KeyCiting	Generically, updating a case or other legal document. Specifically, using KeyCite rather than BCite or Shepard's for this research.
Legislative history	The documents that were generated as a bill became a law.
Legislative Service Commission	The nonpartisan legislative agency that researches issues for the Ohio General Assembly and drafts bills.
LSC	Legislative Service Commission.
Mandatory authority	Primary authority that is binding upon a court. For example, the United States Supreme Court's holding on a federal issue is mandatory authority for all courts in the United States.
Natural-language searching	Similar to Google searching, this type of searching uses a mathematical equation to find the most relevant results.
Non-print published	In Ohio, court of appeals and trial court cases that appear on the Ohio Supreme Court's website are

	called non-print published cases. The court considers all cases that appear on the website to be published, so the term unpublished or unreported is not used.
OJur	*Ohio Jurisprudence*; the Ohio legal encyclopedia.
OAC	Ohio Administrative Code.
OAG	Opinions of the Attorney General of Ohio.
ORC	Ohio Revised Code.
Ordinance	Law enacted by a local entity such as a town or village.
Parallel citations	References for finding a document in various sources. When a legal document appears in more than one source, the document has parallel citations.
Persuasive authority	Authority that is not binding upon a court (e.g., because it is from a different jurisdiction).
Pinpoint citation	A citation to a particular page or paragraph of a document.
Pocket part	Update to a book placed in a pocket inside the back cover of the book.
Primary source	Law produced by government bodies with law-making power. Examples include cases, statutes, and regulations.
Prior history	Anything that happened to a case *before* the citation being updated.
R.C.	A common abbreviation for the Ohio statutory code, Ohio Revised Code.
R.S.	Revised Statutes (Ohio's first statutory codification; were in effect from 1880 to 1910).
Reporter	Sets of books that contain cases in chronological order.
Secondary sources	Writings about the law, such as treatises, law review articles, and Restatements. Although they might

	carry persuasive authority, they are not mandatory authority.
Session law	Statutory law arranged chronologically. Ohio session laws are contained in the *Laws of Ohio*.
Shepardizing	Generically, updating a case or other legal document. Specifically, using Shepard's rather than BCite or KeyCite for this research.
Slip opinion	The actual document produced by the court.
Stare decisis	The principle that courts should follow earlier opinions, ensuring consistency in the law.
Subsequent history	Anything that happened to a case *after* the citation being updated.
Syllabus	A summary of the subsequent opinion. In Ohio, the syllabi of Supreme Court of Ohio opinions are written by the court.
Table of contents	A general list of the subjects covered by a source. Usually found at the beginning of a work.
Terms-and-connectors searching	More precise than natural-language searching, a terms-and-connectors search uses Boolean and proximity operators (e.g., and, not, within the same sentence) to specify the exact relationship between search terms.
Treatise	A work about a specific area of the law (e.g., bankruptcy) that is usually written by an expert in the area. Treatises provide background information, the context surrounding a legal issue, and citations to primary authority.
Uncodified law	A statute that has never been added to the code, either because it is temporary or because it is not of general interest. Notes in the annotated version of a code may refer to important, uncodified law.
Unpublished case	A case that is not selected for publication in one of the print reporter sets. In some jurisdictions, unpublished cases have no precedential value (i.e., they

	are not mandatory authority). In Ohio, cases that appear on the Ohio Supreme Court's website but not in print reporters are called non-print published.
Unreported case	A case that is not selected for publication in one of the print reporter sets. In some jurisdictions, unpublished cases have no precedential value (i.e., they are not mandatory authority).
WebCite	A unique number assigned to every opinion posted on the Ohio Supreme Court's website (e.g., 2015-Ohio-1234).

Appendix C

County and Law School Libraries in Ohio

The following is a list of law libraries in Ohio, excluding law firm libraries. Some county, law library associations, and private law school libraries are not open to the general public. When planning to visit a law library listed below, it may be best to call first to check its access policy. The list is arranged alphabetically by city.

Ada, Ohio
Ohio Northern University
Taggart Law Library
525 S. Main St.
Ada, OH 45810
(419) 772-2239
http://law.onu.edu/library/

Akron, Ohio
Akron Law Library Association
Summit County Court House
209 S. High St., 4th Floor
Akron, OH 44308
(330) 643-2804
https://akronlawlib.summitoh.net

University of Akron Law Library
150 University Ave.
Akron, OH 44325
(330) 972-7330
www.uakron.edu/law/library/

Batavia, Ohio

Clermont County Law Library Association
Clermont County Court House
270 E. Main St.
Batavia, OH 45103
(513) 732-7109
www.clermontlawlibrary.com

Bowling Green, Ohio

Wood County Law Library
1 Courthouse Sq.
Bowling Green, OH 43402
(419) 353-3921
www.co.wood.oh.us/lawlibrary/

Cincinnati, Ohio

Cincinnati Law Library Association
Hamilton County Courthouse
1000 Main St., Rm. 601
Cincinnati, OH 45202
(513) 946-5300
http://lawlibrary.hamiltoncountyohio.gov

University of Cincinnati
Robert S. Marx Law Library
2540 Clifton Avenue
Cincinnati, OH 45221
(513) 556-3016
www.law.uc.edu/library

Cleveland, Ohio

Case Western Reserve University
Judge Ben C. Green Law Library
11075 East Blvd.
Cleveland, OH 44106
(216) 368-5206
http://lawlibrary.case.edu

Cleveland Law Library Association
1 W. Lakeside Ave., 4th Floor
Cleveland, OH 44113
(216) 861-5070
www.clelaw.lib.oh.us

Cleveland State University
Cleveland–Marshall College of Law Library
2121 Euclid Ave.
Cleveland, OH 44115
(216) 687-2253
www.law.csuohio.edu/lawlibrary

Columbus, Ohio

Capital University Law Library
303 E. Broad St.
Columbus, OH 43215
(614) 236-6464
http://law.capital.edu/Law_Library/

Franklin County Law Library
369 S. High St., 10th Floor
Columbus, OH 43215
(614) 525-4971
http://lawlibrary.franklincountyohio.gov

Ohio State University
Michael E. Moritz Law Library
55 W. 12th Ave.
Columbus, OH 43210
(614) 292-6691
http://moritzlaw.osu.edu/library/

Supreme Court of Ohio Law Library
65 S. Front St., 11th Floor
Columbus, OH 43215
(614) 387-9680
http://www.sconet.state.oh.us/LegalResources/LawLibrary/

Dayton, Ohio

Montgomery County Law Library
505 Montgomery County Courts Building
41 N. Perry St.
Dayton, OH 45422
(937) 225-4496
http://www.mcohio.org/government/law_library/

University of Dayton
Zimmerman Law Library
300 College Park
Dayton, OH 45469
(937) 229-2314
http://www.udayton.edu/law/library/index.php

Elyria, Ohio
Lorain County Law Library Association
226 Middle Ave.
Elyria, OH 44035
(440) 329-5567
www.lorainlawlib.org

Findlay, Ohio
Hancock County Law Library
300 S. Main St., 4th Floor
Findlay, OH 45840
(419) 424-7077
http://co.hancock.oh.us/government-services/law-library

Hamilton, Ohio
John F. Holcomb Butler County Law Library
10 Journal Sq., Ste. 200
Hamilton, OH 45011
(513) 887-3455
www.bclawlib.org

Jefferson, Ohio
Ashtabula County Law Library Association
25 W. Jefferson St.
Jefferson, OH 44047
(440) 576-3690
http://courts.co.ashtabula.oh.us/law_library.htm

Mansfield, Ohio
Richland County Law Library Association
50 Park Ave. East
Mansfield, OH 44902
(419) 774-5595

Marietta, Ohio

Washington County Law Library
205 Putnam St.
Marietta, OH 45750
(740) 373-6623, ext. 214
http://www.washingtongov.org/index.aspx?NID=148

Marysville, Ohio

Union County Law Library
215 W. Fifth St., Rm. B-3
Marysville, OH 43040
(937) 645-3000

Painesville, Ohio

Lake County Law Library
47 N. Park Pl.
Painesville, OH 44077
(440) 350-2638
www.lakecountyohio.org/lawlibrary

Ravenna, Ohio

Portage County Law Library
241 S. Chestnut St.
Ravenna, OH 44266
(330) 297-3661

Toledo, Ohio

Toledo Law Association Library
905 Jackson St.
Toledo, OH 43604
(419) 213-4747
www.toledolawlibrary.org

University of Toledo College of Law
LaValley Law Library
2801 W. Bancroft St.
Toledo, OH 43606
(419) 530-2945
http://www.utoledo.edu/law/library/index.html

Warren, Ohio

Trumbull County Law Library Association
120 High St. NW
Warren, OH 44481
(330) 675-2525
http://www.co.trumbull.oh.us/tc_lawlib.html

Xenia, Ohio

Greene County Law Library Association
45 N. Detroit St., 3rd Floor
Xenia, OH 45385
(937) 562-5115
http://www.co.greene.oh.us/index.aspx?NID=411

Youngstown, Ohio

Mahoning Law Library Association
120 Market St., 4th Floor
Youngstown, OH 44503
(330) 740-2295
www.mahoninglawlibrary.org

Appendix D

Selected Legal Writing and Research Texts

Lynn Bahrych & Marjorie Dick Rombauer, *Legal Writing in a Nutshell* (4th ed. 2009)

Mary Beth Beazley, *A Practical Guide to Appellate Advocacy* (4th ed. 2014)

Mary Beth Beazley & Monte Smith, *Legal Writing for Legal Readers* (2014)

Deborah E. Bouchoux, *Legal Research and Writing for Paralegals* (7th ed. 2013)

Charles R. Calleros, *Legal Method and Writing* (7th ed. 2014)

Veda R. Charrow, Myra K. Erhardt & Robert P. Charrow, *Clear and Effective Legal Writing* (5th ed. 2013)

Morris L. Cohen & Kent C. Olsen, *Legal Research in a Nutshell* (11th ed. 2013)

John C. Dernbach et al., *A Practical Guide to Legal Writing & Legal Method* (5th ed. 2013)

Linda H. Edwards, *Legal Writing and Analysis* (3d ed. 2011)

Linda H. Edwards, *Legal Writing: Process, Analysis, and Organization* (6th ed. 2014)

Judith D. Fischer, *Pleasing the Court: Writing Ethical and Effective Briefs* (2d ed. 2011)

Richard K. Neumann, Jr. & Kristin Konrad Tiscione, *Legal Reasoning and Legal Writing: Structure, Strategy, and Style* (7th ed. 2013)

Laurel Currie Oates & Anne Enquist, *The Legal Writing Handbook: Analysis, Research, and Writing* (6th ed. 2014)

Austen L. Parrish & Dennis T. Yokoyama, *Effective Lawyering: A Checklist Approach to Legal Writing and Oral Argument* (2d ed. 2012)

Teresa J. Reid Rambo & Leanne J. Pflaum, *Legal Writing by Design: A Guide to Great Briefs and Memos* (2d ed. 2013)

Jill J. Ramsfield, *Culture to Culture: A Guide to U.S. Legal Writing* (2005)

Mary Barnard Ray & Jill J. Ramsfield, *Legal Writing: Getting It Right and Getting It Written* (5th ed. 2010)

Edward D. Re & Joseph R. Re, *Brief Writing and Oral Argument* (9th ed. 2005)

Amy E. Sloan, *Basic Legal Research: Tools and Strategies* (5th ed. 2012)

Melissa H. Weresh, *Legal Writing: Ethical and Professional Considerations* (2d ed. 2009)

About the Authors

Sara Sampson earned her J.D. from The Ohio State University (OSU) and her M.L.I.S. from Kent State University. She is currently the Assistant Dean for Information Services and Director of Law Library at OSU's Moritz College of Law, where she teaches Legal Analysis and Writing I each fall. She also taught several different legal research and writing courses while working at the law libraries at University of North Carolina and Georgetown University. Dean Sampson began her legal career working as judicial law clerk to judges at the Ohio Fourth District Court of Appeals. She is a member of the Ohio Bar.

Katherine L. Hall earned her J.D. from Indiana University, Bloomington and her M.L.S. from the University of Illinois. From 2001 to 2012, she worked as a reference librarian and then the Assistant Director for Public Services at The Ohio State University Moritz Law Library. She also taught Advanced Legal Research and Ohio Legal Research at OSU's Moritz College of Law. She is currently the Executive Law Librarian and Associate Director of the University of Iowa Law Library. She teaches Advanced Legal Research. She is a member of the California Bar.

Carolyn Broering-Jacobs earned her J.D. from The Ohio State University (OSU). She is currently the Director of Legal Writing at Cleveland–Marshall College of Law. She teaches Legal Research, Writing, and Advocacy; Drafting for the Basic Business Deal; and various additional upper-level research and writing courses. Professor Broering-Jacobs also frequently conducts CLEs and in-house workshops on writing, research, and citation. Before she began teaching, Professor Broering-Jacobs was a litigation associate in the Cleveland office of Baker & Hostetler and clerked for two years for the Honorable Sam H. Bell of the United States District Court for the Northern District of Ohio. She is a member of the Ohio Bar.

Index

Abbreviations, 39–40, 135, 137–138, 148, 150–151, 154, 157, 159–160, 165–169

Administrative law

Administrative codes, 80–81, 83–84

Agencies, 77–78

Agency decisions, 77, 79–80, 86–87

Citing, 87–88

Indexes, 80

Registers, 80, 82, 84–86

Researching federal regulations, 78–80, 83–86

Researching Ohio regulations, 78–82

Researching regulations, 78–86

Updating, 82, 86

Administrative Procedure Act, 77, 85

Administrative Procedure Act, Ohio, 77

Advance Legislative Services, 31

Advance sheets, 65, 165

Agencies, 77–78

Agency decisions, 86–87

American Jurisprudence, 93–94

American Law Reports (ALR), 102–104

American Law Reports Quick Index, 103

Anderson's Annotated Rules Governing the Courts of Ohio, 70

Anderson's Ohio Case Locator, 60

Annotated codes, 19, 71, 129–130, 154

Annotated Model Rules of Professional Conduct, 74

Articles, 98–99

Attorney ethics, 46

Authentication, 13, 136

Baldwin's Ohio Administrative Code Annotated, 80, 82

Baldwin's Ohio Legislative Service, 24–26, 30–31, 117, 121

Baldwin's Ohio Practice Series, 89, 95

Baldwin's Ohio Revised Code Annotated, 19, 33, 70–72, 80, 154

BCite, 56–59, 130, 165

Bieber Dictionary of Legal Abbreviations, 160

Bill analysis, 118, 119, 120

Bill synopsis, 118, 119, 120

Bills, 16, 31, 107, 108–122, 165, 166

Blogs, 12, 99, 100–101

Bloomberg BNA, 39–40, 98, 100

Bloomberg Law, 19, 25, 27, 35, 41, 50–53, 56–58, 76, 96, 98–100, 105, 113, 117
Boolean searching, 41, 50, 168
Bulletin of the General Assembly, 118

Cardiff's Index to Legal Abbreviations, 159–160
Case analysis, 45–48
Cases
  Administrative decisions, 77, 79–80, 86–87
  Citing, 60, 137–146, 150–153
  Federal, 38–40
  Ohio, 36–38
  Online, 36–37, 39, 40–41
  Print digests, 60–67
  Reading and analyzing, 44–48
  Reporters, 35–40
  Researching, 49–56
  Table of Cases, 67
  Updating, 56–60
Certiorari, 8
Chapter 119 agencies, 78
Citation
  ALWD, 12, 21, 33–35, 60, 74, 80, 87–88, 91, 106, 122–123, 134–135, 145, 147–159
  Bluebook, 12, 21, 33–35, 60, 74, 80, 87–88, 91, 106, 122–123, 134–136, 140, 145, 147–159
  Cases
    ALWD and *Bluebook*, 60, 150–153
    Generally, 60
    Ohio Manual of Citation, 60, 137–146
  Constitutions, 21, 155
  Court Rules, 74
  Dictionaries, 147
  Generally, 133–136
  Law review articles, 106, 147, 155, 158–159
  Legislative history documents, 122–123
  Municipal codes, 91, 146–147
  Ohio Manual of Citations, 137–147
  Print or online version, 136
  Regulations, 87–88, 146–147, 153–155
  Secondary sources, 106, 147, 155
  Short form, 147, 151–152
  Statutes
    ALWD and *Bluebook*, 33, 153–155
    Generally, 33
    Ohio Manual of Citation, 33, 146–147
Cities, 89
Code of Federal Regulations, 13, 80, 83–84, 88, 146, 154
Code of Professional Responsibility, 69
Committee hearings, federal, 107, 109, 110, 113–114
Committee hearings, Ohio, 117
Committee prints, 110–111, 113
Committee reports, 107, 110, 112, 113, 116, 117
Compilation of Presidential Documents, 111–112
Compiled legislative history, 111, 113, 114, 165
Complaints, 44–45, 72, 75
Concurring opinion, 44
Congress.gov, 27, 112, 113, 115, 116
Congressional Information Service (CIS), 112

Congressional Record, 111–114, 116, 118

Constitutions
  Amendments, 17
  Citing, 21, 155
  Conventions, 17, 21
  History, 21
  Researching, 17–22
  Updating, 20
Corpus Juris Secundum (CJS), 93, 94
Counties, 89
County courts, 5–7
Court documents, 44, 69, 74–76, 135, 137, 149
Court of Claims, 5–7, 36, 70
Court of Common Pleas, 7–7, 70, 75
Court rules
  Citing, 74
  Local rules, 70
  Researching, 70–73
  Updating, 73
Court structure, 7–9

Decisions, 36–41, 44–48, 77, 79–80, 86–87
Descriptive-Word Index, 63–66
Dicta, 46–47
Dictionaries, citing, 147
Dictionaries, use in research, 10, 44, 55, 159–160
Digest of Enactments, 118
Digests, 50, 53, 55, 60–67, 165
Dissenting opinion, 44
Docket number, 42, 43, 75, 165
Dockets, 74–76

E-CFR, 84, 86
Enabling statute, 77, 81, 84, 165
Executive orders, 111

FDsys, 13, 18, 27, 40, 83–86, 112–114
Federal Appendix, 39
Federal Practice Digest, 62–63
Federal Register, 83–87
Federal Reporter, 39, 150
Federal Supplement, 39, 134
Fiscal note, 118, 120
Form books, 96–98
Full-text searching, 3, 9, 25, 29–30, 49–52, 72, 96, 99, 125

General Assembly, 17, 23–24, 73, 79, 108, 109, 117, 119–120, 122, 165, 166
Gongwer, 100, 119, 122
Google, 12, 50, 99, 100, 114, 166
GPO (Government Publishing Office), 13, 18, 27, 83–85

Hannah Capitol Connection, 119–120
Hannah Report, 100, 119, 122
Headnotes, 43, 47, 53–57, 59, 61–66, 125
HeinOnline, 24, 25, 27, 32, 84, 86, 87, 99, 104, 111, 113–114, 163
Holding, 45–47, 166,
House Journal, 118, 120

Index to Legal Periodicals, 99
Introductory signals, 139–141, 149

Joint Committee on Agency Rule Review (JCARR), 79

KeyCite, 31, 56–60, 73, 82, 86–87, 130, 165, 166, 168

Law journals, 4, 5, 9, 18, 19, 28, 59, 62, 98–99, 106, 125, 134, 136, 147, 149, 155, 158–159, 162, 167

Laws of Ohio, 24, 117, 121, 168

Legal encyclopedias, 4–5, 9, 28, 62, 79, 93–94, 99, 106, 125, 127, 147, 161, 162

Legal newsletters, 98, 99–100

Legal Resource Index, 99

Legal Scholarship Network, 99

LegalTrac, 99

Legislative history
  Acceptance of, 107–108
  Citing, 122–123
  Compiled legislative history, 111, 113, 114, 165
  Use of, 107–108

Legislative process, 107–109

Legislative Service Commission, 82, 118, 120, 161, 166

Legislative Status Sheet, 118

Lexis Advance, 12, 13, 19, 24, 25, 28, 29, 31, 32, 35, 41, 43, 50–58, 66, 70, 73, 76, 80, 82, 84, 86, 87, 90, 96–99, 102–105, 111, 113, 114, 117, 119, 120, 121

Local law
  Citing, 91
  Researching, 89–91
  Updating, 91

Majority opinion, 44

Mandatory authority, 4–5, 74, 125, 166, 167–168, 169

Mayor's Courts, 5–7

Model acts, 93, 105

Municipal codes, 89–91, 146

Municipal Courts, 5–7

National Reporter System, 63

Natural-language searching, 50, 99, 168

Non-print published cases, 36–37, 144–145, 166–167, 169

North Eastern Reporter, 35, 38, 41, 43, 61, 141, 144, 145, 151

Notes of Decision, 19, 26, 84, 102

Official federal code, 12–13, 27, 84, 146, 154

Official federal reporters, 12–13, 35, 39, 146

Official federal session laws, 12–13, 27, 110

Official Ohio code, 12–13, 14, 25

Official Ohio reporters, 12–13, 35, 36–38, 144, 145

Official Ohio session laws, 12–13, 117

Official reporters, 12–13, 35, 145

Ohio Administrative Code, 80–84, 94, 129, 146, 154, 167

Ohio Appellate Reports, 36, 37, 43, 60

Ohio Attorney General opinions, 87, 88

Ohio courts, 5–7

Ohio Courts of Appeals, 5–7

Ohio Lawyer, 100

Ohio Legislature
  See General Assembly

Ohio Miscellaneous Reports, 36, 37, 43, 60, 141, 144

Ohio Monthly Record, 81–82

Ohio Official Reports, 36–37, 143

Ohio Revised Code, 19, 23–26, 28–30, 33, 70–72, 78, 79, 81, 89, 94, 107, 119, 121, 122, 128, 129, 146, 154, 167

Ohio State Bar Association Report, 100

Ohio State Reports, 35, 37, 41–43, 60, 142, 151

Ohio Supreme Court, 7, 16, 21, 35–37, 43, 50, 52, 70, 73, 130, 141, 143, 144, 151, 161

Ordinances, 89, 91, 146

PACER, 76

Page's Bulletin, 24, 31

Page's Ohio Revised Code Annotated, 19, 25, 29, 33, 71, 72, 154

Parallel citation, 63, 138, 141, 145, 146, 167

Pending Opinion Report, 100

Persuasive authority, 4–5, 37, 44, 47, 76, 99, 104, 105, 107, 167, 168

Pinpoint citation, 139, 143, 167

Plagiarism, 134

Pleading and practice forms, 97–98

Plurality opinion, 44

Pocket parts, 31, 63, 65, 95, 105

Popular name table, 27

Primary authority, 4, 9, 11, 25, 28, 29, 43, 78, 99, 101, 125, 166, 168

Prior history, 140, 167

Private laws, 27

Public laws, 27

Regional reporters, 38, 62, 135, 145

Register of Ohio, 82, 84, 87

Research process
  Agency decisions, 86–87
  Agency regulations, 78–86
  Cases, 49–60
  Constitutions, 17–21
  Court rules, 70–73
  Example, 125–132
  Local law, 90–91
  Overview, 3–13

Print digests, 60–67

Statutes, 28–33

Restatements of Law, 5, 93, 103–105, 106, 147, 155, 167

Rules of Professional Conduct, 69–70, 74

Secondary authority, 4, 99

Section 111.15 agencies, 78

Senate Journal, 118, 120

Session laws, 23, 24, 27, 110, 117, 120, 168

Shepardizing
  See Updating

Shepard's, 31, 56–59, 73, 130, 165, 166, 168

Slip opinion, 36, 40, 168

Stare decisis, 46–47, 168

Statutes
  Citing, 33, 146–147, 153–155
  Prior versions, 32–33
  Researching, 28–33
  Surveys, 32
  Updating, 30–31

Statutes at Large, 27, 110, 114

Subject Compilation of State Laws, 32

Subsequent history, 63, 140–141, 153, 168

Supreme Court Reporter (S. Ct.), 39, 135, 138, 146

Supreme courts
  See Ohio Supreme Court and
    United States Supreme Court

Syllabus, 42, 43, 47, 168

TARPP, 10, 11, 71, 126

Terms-and-connectors searching, 50, 52, 168

Topics and key numbers, 55, 60, 63–67, 130

Townships, 89

Transactional forms, 97–98

Transcripts, 75–76, 113, 117

Treatises, 4, 5, 9, 13, 28, 79, 89, 93, 95–97, 106, 125, 147, 167, 168

Uncodified law, 24, 117, 168

Uniform laws, 105

United States Code, 13, 27, 83, 114, 146, 154

United States Code Annotated, 19, 28, 30, 70, 71, 72, 79, 154

United States Code Congressional and Administrative News (USCCAN), 27, 110

United States Code Service, 19, 28, 29, 71, 72, 154

United States Law Week, 39

United States Reports (U.S.), 39, 138, 151

United States Reports, Lawyers' Edition (L. Ed.), 39, 135, 138, 146

United States Supreme Court, 8, 39, 62, 63, 73, 135, 146, 151, 166

Unpublished cases, 39, 168–169

Updating
  Administrative decisions, 86
  Administrative regulations, 82
  Cases, 56–60
  Constitutions, federal, 20
  Constitutions, Ohio, 20
  Court rules, 73
  Municipal codes, 91
  Secondary sources, 96, 97, 104–105
  Statutes, 30–31

Veto, 109, 111

Villages, 89

WebCite, 60, 141–145, 150, 169

West's Code of Federal Regulations General Index, 84

West's Ohio Digest, 60–67

WestlawNext, 12, 13, 19, 20, 24, 25, 28, 29, 31, 32–33, 35, 41, 50–58, 60, 66, 70, 73, 76, 80, 82, 84, 86, 90, 94–100, 102–105, 113, 114–116, 119, 121, 128, 130,

Words & Phrases, 55, 66, 94